Researching children researching the world:
5x5x5=creativity

Researching children researching the world: 5x5x5=creativity

Edited by Susi Bancroft, Mary Fawcett and Penny Hay

Trentham Books

Stoke on Trent, UK and Sterling, USA

Trentham Books Limited

Westview House   22883 Quicksilver Drive
734 London Road   Sterling
Oakhill   VA 20166-2012
Stoke on Trent   USA
Staffordshire
England ST4 5NP

First published 2008

British Library Cataloguing-in-Publication Data
A catalogue record for this book is available from the British Library

ISBN: 978 1 85856 434 0

Designed and typeset by Trentham Print Design Ltd, Chester and printed in Great Britain by The Charlesworth Group, Wakefield.

Contents

CONTENTS

Acknowledgements

Thanks to all the children, young people and adults involved in the research, to all the artists, mentors and cultural centres, to Sightlines Initiative and colleagues from Reggio Emilia.

Special thanks to our Board of Trustees: Anna Craft, Kate Cross, Tamsyn Imison, Sally Jaeckle, Mary Tasker, Steve Ward, Jack Whitehead and Mike Young for their wisdom, to Julia Butler for her care and creative thinking, to Jim Suttie, Phyllida Shaw and Lucinda Roberts for their advocacy and to colleagues from Bath Spa University for supporting the research.

We are grateful for funding from: Arts Council England South West, Esmée Fairbairn Foundation, Bath and North East Somerset, Bristol, North Somerset, Somerset and Wiltshire local authorities, and Awards for All. We have valued previous support from Creative Partnerships and Youth Music. The research would not have been possible without the initial funding from the Wilmington Trust, Arts Council England South West and the National Endowment for Science, Technology and the Arts (NESTA).

Thanks to Sanford UK, Seawhite of Brighton and Specialist Crafts Ltd. for their continuing support with resources.

Thanks to Robin Duckett for inspiring us with the phrase 'researching children researching the world'.

Special thanks to Lily.

Thanks to Reggio Children for permission to use the poem by Loris Malaguzzi 'No way, the hundred is there' in English translation by Lella Gandini from the Catalogue of the Exhibit 'The Hundred Languages of Children' published by Reggio Children in 1996.

5x5x5=creativity
PO Box 3236
Chippenham
Wiltshire
SN15 9DE
www.5x5x5creativity.org

Dedication
Tessa Richardson Jones (1961-2008)

Our lives have been truly enriched by knowing Tess. She had a brightness and vivacity that was dazzling. As an artist, Tess inspired many people with her most beautiful illustrations and she brought her own aesthetic to everything she touched. Tess had an amazing capacity to inspire and engage individuals in their own creativity. She really believed in everyone's capacity to be creative, especially in companionship with others. Tess was totally committed to each person as a unique and special individual. She lit a spark in so many children and adults that she worked alongside. She really listened to children's ideas and had a knack for knowing exactly what to say to make everyone feel good about themselves. She had an instinctive feeling for the important values in all of our lives. Tess's infectious sense of humour and her deep sense of humanity saw her through the difficult bits of life. She was devoted to Jay, Harry and Daisy. We have total admiration for Tess and everything she achieved. She was kind and funny and beautiful, she was a brilliant person. With these thoughts, we dedicate this book to Tess.

Preface

I believe this is an important book for anyone who is interested in developing creativity in education, which in my view means anyone who is interested in the future of education. The book looks in considerable depth into a difficult but vital area of learning, how children use imagination to construct their view of the world. It provides a systematic way of looking at and developing creativity, which is conventionally taken to be inexorably unsystematic, therefore unmeasurable and unreportable.

There is an important principle here: that the capacity to think and create really matter, just as the ability to read and write and calculate do, and we ought to develop that in children for their own well-being and that of society. The book focuses on work with young children but is about us all; it is most certainly about adults learning as well as children. Moreover the approach is for everyone, whatever their background and circumstances.

There are many important ideas in 5x5x5=creativity, inspired by the thinking in Reggio Emilia, but the synthesis and rigour do bring something unique to the UK context. The ideas each have a richness and a history of their own, such as teachers and artists as researchers, children as researchers, bringing the world into the classroom and taking the classroom to the world, respecting children and documenting their learning processes. The working of the central triangle of teacher, artist and cultural setting has great potential, beyond art and into other creative spheres of life.

By involvement in a project like 5x5x5=creativity you learn just how many people and organisations are out there who are willing to work for the good of children; I thank them all. Ultimately what we all want is a better world for children, a world that values childhood.

Mike Young
Chairman of the Board of Trustees, 5x5x5=creativity

Authors

The editorial team, Penny Hay, Susi Bancroft and Mary Fawcett are all experienced authors. Artists, educators and arts professionals also contribute chapters.

Susi Bancroft is an educator and artist. She has been working in education for 25 years. She has a B. Humanities from London University (Froebel Institute) in English and Education, also a PGCE from the Froebel Institute. Her teaching experience covers the primary range with particular expertise in nursery, reception and mixed age early years. Susi spent 4 years as a small school headteacher in Somerset. For 11 years she was with Somerset as an adviser for both Primary Assessment and later for Early Years. She held a South West regional post with the Assessment Advisers Association. Susi has written and contributed to both local and national publications for assessment and early years.

Mary Fawcett (BEd) has been a teacher of nursery and infant children. She was active in the early years of the Preschool Playgroups Association movement and became Chair of Norfolk PPA. At the University of East Anglia she lectured in Early Education and later became the founder and Director of the first degree in Early Childhood Studies at the University of Bristol. Now retired, she works as an educational consultant and has been the lead evaluator of 5x5x5 from its inception.

Penny Hay (MEd) is an artist and educator. Penny is a part-time senior lecturer at Bath Spa University and the Director of Research for 5x5x5=creativity. Previously Penny was a teacher and lecturer in arts education at Goldsmiths College, the Institute of Education (University of London), Roehampton Institute and the University of the West of England. Penny has worked extensively in arts education across the UK and co-ordinated the professional development programme for the National Society for Education in Art and Design (NSEAD). She was instrumental in setting up the National Artist Teacher Scheme with Arts Council England and NSEAD that offers teachers the opportunity to develop their own creative practice. She also coordinated CEDES (Creative Education: Disaffection, Exclusion and Society), an action research project (2003-5), in collaboration with the Centre for Research in Education and Democracy at the University of the West of England. Penny integrates her experience in arts and education with participative action research engaging individuals, institutions and communities.

Contributors

Mandy Adams: cultural centre WOMAD Foundation (World of Music, Art and Dance)

David Allinson: Deputy Headteacher, St Vigor and St John Primary School Chilcompton, mentor, Bishop Henderson Primary School Coleford, Chewton Mendip Primary School, Coxley Primary School, Coordinator for Somerset 5x5x5=creativity

Anna Ashby: educator, Twerton Infant School, Bath

Susi Bancroft: evaluator, 5x5x5=creativity

Kate Cross: Director the egg children's theatre, Bath, linked to St Saviour's Nursery and Infant School and St Stephen's Primary School, Bath

Liz Elders: manager, Kinder Garden Nursery, Bath, mentor, St Saviour's Nursery and Infant School and Marksbury Primary School, Bath

Mary Fawcett: evaluator, mentor, St Stephen's Primary School, Twerton Infant School, Widcombe Acorns Preschool, Bath

Lindsey Fuller: educator, Footprints Nursery, Bristol, Advisory Teacher, Bristol

Ed Harker: Headteacher, St Saviour's Nursery and Infant School, Bath

Penny Hay: Director 5x5x5=creativity, Senior Lecturer in Arts Education, Bath Spa University, mentor, Batheaston Primary School, Combe Down Primary School and Freshford Primary School, Bath

Lesley Hunt: educator, Three Ways School and Lime Grove Special Schools

Deborah Aguirre Jones: artist, Kinder Garden Nursery, Bath, St Julian's Primary School Wellow, Marksbury Primary School, Bath, mentor, St Vigor and St John Primary School, Somerset, St Martins Garden Children's Centre, Bath AND artist

Helen Jury: artist, Three Ways and Lime Grove Special Schools, First Steps Nursery, Twerton Infant School, Bath, mentor, Moorlands Infant School, Bath AND artist

Catherine Lamont Robinson: artist, Exeter House School Wiltshire, St Mary's Infant School, Marlborough, Wiltshire, AND artist

Annabelle Macfadyen: artist, Bishop Henderson Primary School, Coleford, Somerset

Sam Mosley: educator, Freshford Primary School, Bath

Catharine Naylor: artist, Freshford Primary School, Bath

Gill Nicol: artist, mentor

Tessa Richardson Jones: artist, Acorns Pre-school, Freshford Primary School, Twerton Infant School, Bath

Jayne Rochford Smith: educator, Twerton Infant School, Bath

Sandy Shepard: educator, Bishop Henderson Primary School, Somerset

Jane Southwell: educator, Moorlands Infant School, Bath, Advisory Teacher, Bath and North East Somerset

Andrea Sully: educator, Four Acres Nursery and Primary School, Bristol, Adviser, North Somerset

Karen Wallis: artist, Moorlands Infant School, Bath, AND artist

Introduction

Penny Hay

Creativity is an essential life skill but what does this really mean? What are the most effective ways of supporting creative development? How can artists enable creative thinking in adults and children? Children are born equipped with amazing creative capacities. These include the powerful drive to explore, hypothesise, make connections and communicate ideas. 5x5x5=creativity is discovering how this creativity can be supported in children's and adults' lives, both in educational settings and in their homes.

5x5x5 started as a conversation around a kitchen table, a discussion focused on the potential for engaging young people in philosophical enquiries around contemporary art practice. Following a pilot with *Bath Area Network for Artists*, 5x5x5=creativity originally involved five educational settings, five artists and five cultural centres (galleries, theatres, music centres) working in dynamic, researchful partnership to support young children's creativity working in a multi-professional way.

Today **5x5x5=creativity** is a well-established arts-based action research organisation that collects evidence about children's life-wide creative capacities in order to support and develop these effectively. Recently, thanks to support from the Esmée Fairbairn Foundation, it has become an independent not-for-profit limited company with charitable status. It is influenced by the creative educational approach of early years settings in Reggio Emilia in Northern Italy and the Creative Foundation (led by Sightlines Initiative) in the UK, but has developed it own identity. The influence of Reggio Emilia is world-wide but there is very little literature which reports on other cultures' approach to the fundamental principles identified in their practice. The system of values, the structure and the practice of 5x5x5 are very powerful.

From seven years' experience in over 55 settings (schools and preschools) in five local authorities we want to share our discoveries. We would like to whet others' appetites and to offer the processes we have found so successful in developing creative learning. We aim to inspire and transform both personal and professional practice.

Since the outset, our work has been informed by many questions, such as:

How can we develop creative and reflective methodologies to support children's enquiries about the world?

Do we share or 'uphold' our creative values? How do we make these values transparent?

How can we support children's dispositions and creative behaviours?

How can artists model the creative process alongside children?

How can we start with children's ideas in a content led curriculum?

How can we transform the culture of education to prioritise the child?

What kind of innovative practices can be integrated into mainstream policy?

What do we mean by creative learning?

What does a creative teacher do? What does a creative learner do?

How is children's creativity nurtured and developed?

How can we generate creative learning environments?

What is the balance between structure and freedom?

What are the values of an effective partnership?

How can we collect meaningful documentation?

How open are we to the concepts of transformation as a result of dialogue?

What models of creative learning may be constructed in the future?

What might those creative pedagogies look like?

We hope this book will shed light on these questions. The vision of 5x5x5 is to develop creative reflective practice and influence systemic change. As a group of researchers, we are learning together in environments of enquiry, challenging orthodoxies and developing new ways of thinking.

This book attempts to capture the complexity of the process involved in 5x5x5: its structure, values, intellectual depth and aesthetic qualities. Artists, educational settings, cultural centres, arts organisations, families, local authorities and universities are all involved in this process.

We offer an accessible multi-layered study of the work including case studies, interviews with artists, journals and discussions of the strategies used in the research. The philosophical foundations of the approach involving a fundamental shift in thinking about children, their learning and creativity are explored. Several colleagues have contributed chapters so there will be refreshingly varied approaches. 5x5x5 offers a strategic approach that is child-focused and long-term in contrast to much other practice. The book aims not only to share our practical and philosophical experience but also to encourage more people to work in this creative way.

The book is rich in information. Chapter 1 explores the philosophical framework, based on creativity as a democratic notion and valuing children as competent creative learners. Chapter 2 addresses the theoretical and political context for the research, drawing on relevant literature, related research and recent government documentation. Chapter 3 discusses the 'invisible framework' that makes the collaborative research so successful and the challenges of making 5x5x5 work in practice: sections include the practice of documentation as a research tool; the creative and reflective cycle of research; collaboration and partnership; the role of the mentor together with the ongoing evaluation of the research and integrated professional development. Chapter 4 describes illuminative case studies, vignettes of transformative learning stories and lines of enquiry in the research (learning dispositions; fantasy play; the outdoors; musical intelligences; creative digital technologies). Chapter 5 offers different perspectives with personal and professional reflections from educators and parents on 5x5x5=creativity. Chapter 6 focuses on the artists' role in 5x5x5=creativity, the artists' network development (AND) and includes excerpts from an artist's journal. Chapter 7 looks at key aspects of learning for the cultural centres involved in 5x5x5=creativity. Chapter 8 is both reflective and forward looking and offers a wide range of considerations for the future and the legacy of 5x5x5=creativity. We hope the book will guide you to dream and imagine a world of new possibilities.

> True education flowers at the point when delight falls in love with responsibility. If you love something, you want to look after it. (Philip Pullman, *Saturday Guardian*, January 22, 2005)

1

Our philosophical framework

Penny Hay

Imagine a world where our children are engaged in serious creative play, where their environments are full of space and light ... where adults are companions in the children's enquiries about the world ... creative adults who show a deep respect for children's ideas, theories and fascinations.

5x5x5=creativity is an independent, arts-based action research organisation that aims to collect evidence about children's life-wide creative capacities.

It involves groups of artists, educators and cultural centres working in partnership to support children in their exploration and expression of ideas. 5x5x5 is inspired by the approach in Reggio Emilia, Northern Italy and Sightlines Initiative (the UK reference point for Reggio Children) but has also developed a unique identity. Reggio Emilia is an example of sustained local innovative practice. It is a city in which the nature of meaningful enquiry has been an ongoing focus of exploration for more than sixty years.

> All that we need to know about children, for children, is best learned from the children themselves. (Loris Malaguzzi, founder and for many years director of Reggio Emilia preschools, in Edwards *et al*, 1998)

Conceived in 2000 in Bath and North East Somerset (B&NES), 5x5x5 originally involved five educational settings, five artists and five cultural centres working in partnership. This initiative built on the *Making Art Work* (Hay, 2001) research that investigated the quality of arts education provision in the Bath area. The recommendations of the report included the value of partnerships between contemporary artists, arts organisations and educational institutions to develop more creative approaches to learning based on philo-

1

sophical enquiry. A moment of serendipity and synchronicity helped to bring together the authors of this book – we all have a commitment to the power of the arts to be transformative in our lives and a deep interest in child development.

Seven years on, 5x5x5=creativity is now established as an independent charity, 55 research settings have been involved across five Local Authorities: Bath and North East Somerset, Bristol, North Somerset, Somerset and Wiltshire.

Our research is based on a view of all children as creative, competent and with potential, 'an image of a child as strong, powerful, and rich in resources, right from the moment of birth' (Rinaldi, 1998). The adults see themselves as 'researching children researching the world.' Engaging in such research provides rich possibilities for working creatively with children and cultural communities, addressing national issues about the creative arts in society.

The aims of the research were originally:

- to demonstrate ways in which creativity and innovation can be fostered in and with young children

- to influence educational practice and policy by establishing creativity as an essential foundation of learning

- to share the findings as widely as possible, creating a legacy for the future.

The objects of 5x5x5=creativity, set out in our charity's Memorandum and Articles of Association, are the advancement of education in particular by:

- working in partnership with educators and artists, and with museums, galleries, theatres and other artistic and cultural settings to support children in their exploration, communication and expression of creative ideas

- producing and disseminating research and guidance on creative values, relationships, environments and dispositions in order to help develop children as confident, creative thinkers

- providing integrated training and mentoring for educators, artists and those involved in cultural settings.

Our ambition is to change society's understanding of creativity and centralise its place in learning and teaching. Our vision is to give children and adults the means to develop their creativity, no matter what their background or circumstances.

We are committed to promoting access and excellence and believe that everyone, regardless of their age, gender, ability, or personal circumstances, should have access to the highest quality professional creative experiences. Through their involvement in 5x5x5=creativity, children are able to develop life-wide creative capacities and become confident, creative learners in every aspect throughout their lives. 'These children are the ones who give shape to things, they are not just destined to submit ...' (Malaguzzi in Edwards *et al*, 1998).

5x5x5=creativity philosophy

In essence the key philosophical principles of 5x5x5 are:

- ■ Children are seen as innate and creative knowledge builders, explorers and co-constructors of their learning

- ■ Educators and artists are enablers and companions in the children's learning within a culture of listening

- ■ Learning is focused on the process of the children's explorations, not the end product

- ■ Documenting children's learning journeys is our method for evaluating and reflecting upon the children's thinking and learning

- ■ The development of a creative learning community of teachers, artists, co-workers in cultural centres, parents and children

- ■ Involving family and community in life-long learning

Children need the freedom to appreciate the infinite resources of their hands, their eyes and their ears, the resources of forms, materials, sounds and colours. They need the freedom to realise how reason, thought and imagination can create continuous interweaving of things, and can move and shake the world. (Malaguzzi, *ibid*)

A creative and reflective pedagogy

Critical reflective evaluation of action is at the heart of the 5x5x5 research. In 5x5x5 we have recognised that the quality of the work depends on a creative and reflective pedagogy. A continuous cycle maintains a rich level of thinking that keeps 'research as a habit of mind' (Moss, 2003).

We want to make explicit and transparent the values that underpin our research. Emphasis is placed on children taking responsibility alongside adults for their learning, asking good questions, making choices and being curious about the world. In 5x5x5 we are supporting children as independent, creative and reflective thinkers involved in rich and authentic learning. We want to respond to all five of the outcomes of *Every Child Matters*: to improve the life chances of children through developing their confidence in themselves as creative learners, thinkers and problem solvers with higher levels of motivation and engagement in their learning. Loris Malaguzzi wrote:

> Once children are helped to perceive themselves as authors or inventors, once they are helped to discover the pleasures of inquiry, their motivation and interest explode. ... to disappoint the children deprives them of possibilities that no exhortation can arouse in later years. (Edwards *et al*, 1998)

Careful listening, observations and reflection on children's learning give shape to pedagogical thought. Inspired by the educational culture in Reggio Emilia, the research in 5x5x5 has generated a sound evidence base for child-initiated learning framed by supportive adults. As adults, we are co-creators of knowledge. In 5x5x5 the adults' role is to create a context in which the children's curiosity, theories and research can be legitimated and listened to. Listening also involves observation, documentation and interpretation to make learning visible. Collaborative reflection holds and explores that cognitive tension so possibilities can emerge: this cognitive tension leads to joint enquiry and collaborative meaning making, which defines the quality of the research.

There is also the 'emotionally moving sense of the search for meaning' which makes research 'contemporary and alive' (Rinaldi in Giudici *et al*, 2001). It was Malaguzzi who inspired in Reggio a belief in the importance of research as an integral part of everyday life. Peter Moss (2003) describes how Malaguzzi and Reggio have also provided us with a powerful tool for making schools spaces for the practice of democratic political practice: pedagogical documentation.

> This method for making pedagogical work visible and therefore subject to interpretation and critique welcomes difference and confrontation, multiple perspectives and divergent interpretations. Pedagogical documentation serves several purposes: evaluation, where evaluation is understood as a democratic process of meaning making rather than the managerial assessment of quality; learning about learning, through adopting a researching approach.

> Behind the practice I believe is the ethical concept of a transparent school and transparent education. Reggio's 'pedagogy of listening' provides one way in which this important shift can be made. For a pedagogy of listening means listening to thought – the ideas and theories, questions and answers of children – treating thought seriously and with respect, struggling to make meaning from what is said, without preconceived ideas of what is correct or appropriate.

Reggio is seen as a complex of workshops or laboratories, where children and adults are constantly experimenting, inventing and welcoming the new and unknown. Howard Gardner, working with *Project Zero* at Harvard University in Boston USA, looks at two key issues from Reggio Children. Firstly, the notion of 'deep documentation': capturing why and how something happened rather than just a traditional descriptive narrative. Secondly, the notion of a 'gallery of learning': how to represent that documentation and evaluation in order to recreate the learning experiences for new audiences (Gardner in Giudici *et al*, 2001).

> Documentation invites enquiry about children's thinking ...documentation is a research report used to enhance discourse rather than a record of a past event. (Edwards *et al*, 1998).

Our 5x5x5 research projects have not been pre-structured, but have emerged through close collaboration, dialogue and observation. They have developed as interactive experiences, the adults learning from and supporting the children in their development as makers and creators, adults observe and listen to children's interests, hypotheses and motivations. The approach also requires attention and commitment for us all to learn about ourselves as learners together, to understand and develop a common pedagogy, and to give the time, space and attention to engaging in formative research that is illuminating and qualitative.

> The potential for every child is stunted if the endpoint of learning is formulated in advance. (Rinaldi, 1998)

Structure of 5x5x5=creativity

In the UK there are an increasing number of artist/educator collaborations that aim to facilitate creative educational practice. 5x5x5 is exploring in detail the possible ways of making this happen. It has a unique structure for investigating the requirements of successful creative and reflective practice.

Working with Sightlines Initiative we have developed a clear set of guidelines that underpin our research:

- Artists and educators collaborate in engaging with children's own explorations of their world, and focus on supporting communication between children

- The artist is a creative enabler, who works with the educators in their development of ongoing, creative learning environments

■ The triangular collaboration of artist, educator and cultural centre develops and broadens the educators' understanding and development of creative learning processes and environments

■ We are committed to exploration of the opportunities and possibilities of working in collaboration with cultural centres

■ Representation, or creation, is seen as a tool for deeper comprehension, or exchange of ideas, rather than as an ultimate goal

■ Close attention to the creative process in 5x5x5 aims to deepen our understanding of creativity

■ The work with the children and all the adults involved is supported throughout by evaluation and reflective processes

■ 5x5x5 is consistently aware of current national and international educational research and is searching for opportunities to contribute to debate, research and networking.

This approach demands practitioners who see themselves as co-researchers, working alongside the child in a shared spirit of enquiry – practitioners who have the confidence to work flexibly and responsively in the best interests of every child. It is a sophisticated and challenging approach, but is also exciting, bringing back the sparkle to the learning experience. (Sally Jaeckle, Regional Director for the Foundation Stage, DCSF South West and 5x5x5=creativity Trustee)

Principles of 5x5x5=creativity in practice
A pedagogy of listening

If we believe that children possess their own theories, interpretations, and questions, and that they are co-protagonists in the knowledge-building process, then the most important verb in educational practice is no longer to talk, to explain, or to *transmit*, but to *listen*. (Rinaldi, 1998)

Underpinning all the work in 5x5x5 is the 'pedagogy of listening' (*ibid*). Everyone's worth and their contributions are recognised; children's ideas are heard and supported. When children are listened to and offered a creative environment they 'take off', they experience a sense of ownership and satisfaction that is lasting.

The best conditions for thinking, if you really stop and notice are not tense. They are gentle. They are quiet. They are unrushed. They are stimulating but not competitive. They are encouraging. They are paradoxically both rigorous and nimble. Attention, the act of listening with respect and fascination is the key to a thinking environment. When you are listening to someone, much of the quality of what you are hearing is your effect on them. Your attention, your listening is that important. (Kline, 1998)

A creative and reflective cycle

In practical terms 5x5x5 starts by observing and listening to the children, followed by a reconnaissance of the possibilities, experimenting with different approaches and continual evaluation of the outcomes. The evaluation process throughout 5x5x5 gives opportunities for a creative and reflective cycle at all levels (see chapter 3).

Child-focused processes (not products)

The whole process by which children explore, think, represent and discuss is the focus, not the final products. It is easy to be impressed by tangible objects constructed by children rather than the thought-processes that inform them. Too often educational settings offer adult-directed art activities with little thought or imagination expected from the child. Creative interventions and provocations from the artists are catalysts for the children's own thinking and meaning making. When children have the opportunities to play with ideas in different contexts, they discover new connections and understanding. Adult support in this process of enquiry enhances their ability to think critically and ask good questions.

The hundred languages of children

The phrase, 'the hundred languages of children' comes from a poem by Loris Malaguzzi. Valuing children's expression through all forms – verbal, non-verbal, through movement, music, drawing, painting, constructing, using technical equipment such as cameras and computers – helps us grasp and respond to children's thinking. More than this, offering different forms of representation to children opens up learning opportunities for all. This is an example of inclusive education in action. In Reggio Emilia every class has its own *atelier* or workshop, a place to explore the 'hundred languages'. Our evidence is that children spontaneously and creatively connect all forms of thinking and expressive representation.

Documentation

Careful observations and documentation of children's words will provide insight into their ideas and understandings. Documentation is a reflective process that makes flexible planning possible and modifies the teaching and learning relationship. It informs our way of being with children – how we 'see' them, respond and relate to them – and ensures children or childhood is not 'anonymous'. It improves our professional knowledge of how children think, feel and learn. It involves gathering and interpreting the children's learning experiences using all possible means, visual and written. The purpose of the documentation is not to simply gather material for a display, it is central to our research. All the material documentation is examined through dialogue with colleagues, themes found and future possibilities developed. From the recorded sequences of learning, 'learning stories' are identified and displayed for children, parents and other colleagues to share (see chapter 3 on documentation) review and revisit.

Continuous professional development

5x5x5=creativity has a dual personal development focus: on the participating children and on the education and arts practitioners. All the participants (artists, educators and colleagues from the cultural centres) take part in continuous professional development, an integral part of the project – RED days are identified for Reflection, Exchange and Dialogue. Colleagues present their research, learning stories and discuss challenges. Wider professional development continues throughout the research and also involves whole staff teams and the parents. Involvement in a creative learning community is also made possible through the partnership with Bath Spa University who offer accreditation for the research and a regional ReFocus group affiliated to Sightlines Initiative. The continuing professional development of 5x5x5 practitioners – in both education and arts – is essential to effecting sustainable change in policy and practice (see chapter 3).

Collaboration with parents and the community

Parents are the first educators of their children and of course continue in this role. Their involvement in 5x5x5 – for example as documenters or participants in professional development – enriches the experience for everyone. The more we share children's interests together with their families, the more we can all understand and support them. Children are based within their own communities and bring their family culture into their educational setting. Collaboration with parents is a vital aspect of the research. As adults it is our role to facilitate and support children's depth of learning: by respecting children and taking time to make observations and connections with the children's thinking, we can refine our own efforts in supporting their learning more effectively (see chapters 3 and 5).

Democracy and participation

This research depends on collaborative working at all levels: children together, professional colleagues (artists, educators and colleagues from cultural centres), parents and the community with each other and all these groups with the children. All are seen as co-learners and co-constructors of knowledge, forming creative, collaborative and reflective learning communities. All aspects of 5x5x5 are documented and thus made transparent and accessible to all participants. Everyone's voice is heard.

Rigour in research

5x5x5 is focused on exploring children researching and representing the world together, with adults supporting them. Our main focus is adults' scaffolding of children's enquiries and hypotheses about the world through creative values, behaviours and environments. We have faith in the creative capacity and competence of everyone, children and adults. Deep probing enquiries challenging each other's perspectives open up the creative possibilities in children's learning. As Carrie Beckett of Pitton Preschool says: '... it's like putting on a pair of glasses and seeing everything much sharper and in focus'.

Respect for children's ideas

All the adults, artists, educators and cultural colleagues have demonstrated their commitment in 5x5x5 to work based on a deep respect for children. The children see themselves as researchers, as protagonists in their own learning. Time, space and attention are given to supporting and developing children's hypotheses and theories about the world. Focusing on children's questions, schemas and learning dispositions allows us to negotiate the lines of enquiry. When children collaborate in small groups this allows for more significant, powerful learning to take place alongside interested adults, to re-evaluate their thinking and theories through conversation and dialogue.

> This exciting enterprise is as much about the transformation of teachers as it is about the transformation of children. The teachers involved over the last seven years now have an exceptional quality and rigour of educational thought. They are true 'lead learners': excited about and skilled in, not only their own learning, but in scaffolding the learning of others: children, parents, artists and members of the enlightened participating cultural communities. (Dame Tamsyn Imison, education strategist and 5x5x5=creativity Trustee)

The four elements of our research in 5x5x5=creativity

From all the learning journeys over the last seven years we have collected vast quantities of documentation at many levels. This store-house of experience is only valuable if we can share it with others and if we can raise the understanding of creativity in education much more widely and contribute to the understanding of creativity in our culture.

We are collecting evidence about the impact and educational effect our research can have in relation to the revised *Early Years Foundation Stage* and the promise of *Excellence and Enjoyment* and *Every Child Matters.*

Everyone's research radiates from this central idea that we are researching ourselves, researching the children, researching the world. Our observations of the children lead us to 'follow the smoke' and look closely for their fascinations, interests and exchanges.

Our own thinking frame has evolved identifying four elements of our research:

Creative values (the competence and strength of the child, pedagogy of listening)

Creative relationships (attentive, respectful adults and children working collaboratively)

Creative environments (both physical and emotional)

Creative behaviours and dispositions (supporting creative thinking and learning dispositions; holistic learning)

We ourselves are creating a new language to describe creativity – these definitions are not fixed. Everyone is contributing to the construction of meanings. When we look through our documentation we find examples that build our knowledge of these elements.

> I am convinced ... that the effect of documentation (documents, notes, slides, and recordings) is not limited to making visible that which is, but on the contrary, by making an experience visible, documentation enables the experience to exist and thus makes it sharable and open to the 'possibles' (possible interpretations, multiple dialogues among children and adults). Therefore, I believe that narrating the learning process requires the use of verbal and visual languages not only in a narrative and analytical way, but also in a poetic, metaphorical, musical, physical, and dramatic sense.

> In other words, in order to make a learning experience possible – and therefore to make it a conscious form of learning that can also be narrated – processes and language should be closely interwoven, so as to support each other reciprocally and to support the quality of the learning experience itself. What we actually have to document (and therefore bring into existence) is the 'emotionally moving' sense of the search for the meanings of life that children and adults undertake together – a poetic sense that metaphorical, analogical, and poetic language can produce and thereby express in its holistic fullness. (Rinaldi in Giudici *et al*, 2001)

5x5x5=creativity offers such an invisible structure for teachers to work along-side artists and cultural centres to critically analyse, reflect on and appraise their values in relation to their pedagogical practice. In the spirit of Reggio Emilia, children can become active citizens as protagonists in their own learning, to contribute to a negotiated curriculum and an education that be-longs to them in a society with a vision of children who can act and think for themselves.

> 5x5x5=creativity helps improve the life chances of children by developing their con-fidence in themselves as creative learners, thinkers and problem solvers whilst in-spiring higher levels of motivation and engagement in their learning. (Sally Jaeckle, Director for the Foundation Stage, DCSF and 5x5x5=creativity Trustee)

5x5x5=creativity is now nationally recognised as a long-term research project that is contributing to an international, critical debate about how to build an educational culture that can change lives.

2

The wider context

Mary Fawcett and Penny Hay

a) What literature does 5x5x5 draw on?

Creativity should not be considered a separate mental faculty, but a characteristic of our way of thinking, knowing and making choices.

Creativity becomes more visible when adults try to be more attentive to the cognitive processes of children than to the results they achieve. (Malaguzzi in Edwards *et al*, 1998)

The work of 5x5x5=creativity during the last seven years has not been taking place in a vacuum. Other research and literature, mostly from the UK, has encouraged us in our own research. 5x5x5 values and invites openness and reciprocity within the wider research community. Some revealing insights, fresh perspectives and validation of our philosophy and approach have been brought together in this chapter.

The 5x5x5 approach to research is dealt with in more detail in chapter 3. Rinaldi (in Giudici *et al*, 2001) describing the concept in Reggio Emilia writes:

Research, in this sense, is used to describe the paths of individuals and groups in the direction of new universes of possibility. Research as the disclosure and the revelation of an event. Research as art: research exists, as it does in art, within the search for the being, the essence, and the sense of things.

In 5x5x5 we explore the notion of creativity and creative thinking as 'a function of intelligence' (Robinson, 2001), a 'state of mind' (Lucas in Craft *et al*, 2001) or 'going beyond the conventional agreed' (Craft, 2000) and one of the 'higher cognitive functions' (Gardner, 1999). Koestler (1999) defines creativity as 'the ability to make connections between previously unconnected ideas'. Csikszentmihalyi (1997, 2002) uses the phrase 'in the flow' to describe immersion in the creative process; a state he characterises by intense concentration, absorption, pleasure and lack of awareness of time passing.

Craft (2002), drawing on *All Our Futures* (NACCCE, 1999), describes creativity as 'Imagination and purpose; originality; value; questioning and challenging; making connections and seeing relationships; envisaging what might be; exploring ideas, keeping options open; reflecting critically on ideas, actions and outcomes'.

The term creative in 'creative learning' signals the involvement of pupils in 'being innovative, experimental and inventive' (Jeffrey, 2005), and the learning signifies that pupils 'engage in aspects of ... intellectual enquiry'.

Recent UK government initiatives embrace the idea of creativity and creative thinking as central to learning. These include *All Our Futures* (1999), *Excellence and Enjoyment* (2003), *Primary National Strategy* (2004), *Creative Partnerships* (2005), *Every Child Matters* (2006) and the new *Early Years Foundation Stage* (2007).

In the research with 5x5x5=creativity, a framework of four areas has emerged from our enquiries over the last few years: creative values, creative relationships, creative environments and creative learning dispositions and behaviours are key themes that underpin our research.

Creative values

Children seen as powerful learners

In common with 5x5x5, Hart *et al* (2004) present an unshakeable belief in everybody's capacity to learn, rather than the concept of being born with fixed ability. *Learning without Limits* (*ibid*) makes a powerful statement about the transformative possibilities of education. The authors are deeply concerned that educational practice in the UK (and USA) is largely dominated by judgements based on the notion of inborn ability. In other countries, educators are not fatalistic about children's capacities – every child is perceived as having potential from birth. The greatest negative impact of adults holding narrow, fixed ideas about a child is on the child's own self-perceptions. It reduces the young person's chances of developing self-confidence and skills competence. The book includes case studies of pedagogy that demonstrate the concept of 'transforming learning capacity'. In the schools involved, the educators were intent on 'building confidence and emotional security, strengthening feelings of competence and control, increasing young people's sense of acceptance and belonging' (*ibid*).

Children as people now

Children are people now, not adults in preparation. Doddington and Hilton (2007) in their recent book *Child-centred Education: Reviving the creative tradition* add to the debate from historical and philosophical perspectives. The writers note: 'childhood is *a time in itself* [their italics] and not 'a time of preparation'. A view of childhood as preparation for future adulthood is an old assumption. These researchers remind us that it is problematic to attempt to predict what that future might be either for society or individuals. Child-centred educationalists claim 'rich educational experience in the present should be our main concern.'

Democracy and participation

Burnard *et al* (2006) documents ways in which practitioners promote an ethos in which children have a significant voice in decisions. Recognising children's capacity for genuine and active participation links to our first value of believing in children's competence.

In Reggio children are recognised as bearers of rights, reflecting the provision of consistent values building upon democratic and equal learning partnerships. The child is central to this process, 'negotiation' is valued over 'instruction', views and opinions are sought, and children are active protagonists of their own learning.

5x5x5=creativity depends on collaborative working at all levels (chapter 3): of children together, professional colleagues (artists, educators and colleagues from cultural centres), of parents and the community with each other and all these groups with the children. All aspects of 5x5x5 are documented and thus made transparent and accessible to all participants.

Little c creativity

Anna Craft's writing about creativity in education (2002) highlights the notion of little 'c' creativity which is very close to the definition we have used in 5x5x5. She states that creativity is life-wide and life-long. Everyone has the capacity for little 'c' creativity, it is not just the preserve of the genius. Our evidence in 5x5x5=creativity is that children spontaneously and creatively connect all forms of thinking and expressive representations, demonstrating their use of the *hundred languages* of children.

Adults and children together

John Matthews (2002) writes

> The best teachers relate to very young children as fellow learners. A teacher is an adult companion to the child on an intellectual adventure ... This sincere engagement ... helping them develop a particular mode of thinking which is called meta-cognition – the ability to think about one's own thinking.

Craft too has picked out the reciprocity of children and adults as a significant value (2006). Both teachers and children should have the opportunity to be autonomous according to Doddington and Hilton (2007). Anning and Ring (2004) describe how children show capability, confidence and independence by demonstrating 'thinking in process' and how adults are co-constructors of learning, engaging appropriately with the child's interests in order to support learning rather than dominating and over directing. This is central to the work in 5x5x5=creativity.

> Our most important and valuable ideas are the products of shared enthusiasms and ambitions learned in the joy and hurt of companionship. We have to recognise children's eagerness to know, and then run with them in exercising it. Educators, especially, must think about this human sharing, about how different people of any age, with their different experiences and different purposes, can act and think together. (Trevarthen, 2006)

Play and flow

'Playing, experimenting children come to new knowledge in sensual, affective and active ways that enable them to understand its substance' (Doddington and Hilton, 2007). Historically play has been valued as a vital way of children learning about the world. McMillan, Isaacs and Dewey are quoted as examples by Doddington and Hilton (2007). In play, children reach their highest levels of thinking according to Vygotsky (1978). The deep concentration which is often observed in children's play is an example of 'flow' (Cziksentmihalyi, 2002). Bruce (1991) talks of free flow exploratory play as the combination of ideas, feelings and relationships with the development of increased competence and control. This commitment to 'play as a child's work' (Gussin Paley, 2004) is a key area of 5x5x5 research.

An environment of enquiry

> ... the British National Curriculum provides the most detailed, instrumental and narrowly defined list of subjects and skills ever conceived, all of which enclose and formalise 'school learning' even for the youngest children. (Doddington and Hilton, 2007)

16

The very existence of a National Curriculum makes the assumption that knowledge can be packaged and passed on. However, rather than transmitting knowledge it is better that teachers 'enable children to become independent thinkers, not always to correct them, to allow them to probe information and problems and experience in order to establish sound beliefs, decisions and judgements' (*ibid*). The school should be a place for enquiry, for the construction of knowledge, about formulating questions and seeking answers to those genuine problems. Possibility thinking, which is fundamental to creativity, depends on the ability to ask questions (Burnard *et al*, 2006).

The significance of the whole body
'The mind does not function without a body. We are all embodied – feeling and physicality are not separate' (Welton in Doddington and Hilton, 2007) '... all lived experience, what some have called our 'life world', is concretely real and initially pre-theoretical, but from the beginning, because we are socially embedded from babyhood, our experiences and understandings are socially constructed' (*ibid*). The authors have consolidated our own views on what counts as the 'whole child' and offer a version that includes an emphasis on personal authenticity, meaningful understanding and the importance of children being able to develop a strong sense of themselves through their education.'

Creative relationships
Creative relationships are crucial to 5x5x5. We draw on several social constructivist theories and models of education and have been informed by Matthews' (1999) research into children's theories of the world and how they construct meaning through their own art making.

Pringle (2003) emphasises the role of dialogue and discussion in developing creative conversations between adults and children. In this context the artist is seen as a creative enabler and facilitator of possibilities. Katz (1993) describes how young children benefit from frequent, continuous, contingent, sustained interactions. Children need opportunities to engage in cycles of interactions and feedback, and in revisiting experiences to deepen their learning. Katz warns us never to undervalue children's intellectual powers and motivations during our work in helping children to develop the 'intellectual habits of mind' that they will need throughout their lives.

A major UK longitudinal study funded by the DfES, *Effective Pedagogy in the Early Years* studied the most effective pedagogical strategies that were being applied in the Foundation Stage to support the development of young children's skills, knowledge and attitudes, and ensure they make a good start at school (Siraj-Blatchford *et al*, 2002). One of the most significant findings is the importance of 'sustained shared thinking'. The report defines this as happening when an adult works with 'two or more individuals in an intellectual way to solve a problem, clarify a concept, evaluate activities, extend a narrative, etc.' In fact though, this type of adult/child interaction was rarely observed in their study.

Craft (2002) discusses creativity, encompassing personal effectiveness. Adult pedagogies influencing creativity are 'choice and ownership; personal relevance; reflective time; purposeful outcomes; stimulating environment'.

Jeffrey and Woods (2003) define pedagogical strategies and explore notions of ownership, relevance, innovation and control and co-participation where control is handed back to the learner. Burnard *et al* (2006) identify a number of distinct but interlinked core features of learners' and teachers' engagement which are valued and fostered in each setting: posing questions, play, immersion, innovation, being imaginative, self-determination and risk-taking. Craft, Burnard, Grainger *et al* (2006) define strategies found to be important in pedagogical approaches to creativity that include the use of space and time, fostering self-esteem and self-worth, offering learners mentors in creative approaches, involving children in higher level thinking skills, encouraging the expression of ideas through a wide variety of expressive and symbolic media, encouraging the integration of subject areas through topics holding meaning and relevance to the children's lives.

Malaguzzi (1993) holds the 'image of the child as rich in potential, strong, powerful, competent', that this is not in isolation but is relational: 'and, most of all, connected to adults and other children ... we must know that children ... extract and interpret models from adults when the adults know how to work, discuss, think, research, and live together.'

Creative environments

In 5x5x5=creativity we have been researching children's creative learning dispositions and behaviours within the creative environments that we adults offer them (Cremin *et al*, 2006). Harrington (1990) brings the factors of process, people and physical environment together within a theoretical framework of the 'creative ecosystem'. The components of Harrington's ecosystem in which creativity may flourish are an atmosphere or 'ambience' of creativity; stimulation; opportunities for play; easy access to resources; mentors and role models; permission and support; motivation and encouragement; information and open-ended tasks.

Reggio Emilia preschools term the environment the 'third teacher'. Specifically the *atelier* contains a wide range of media and materials for fostering creativity and learning through projects, and provides a place for children to learn and use a variety of techniques. Each school also employs an *atelierista*, a teacher specifically trained in the arts, who collaborates with the classroom teachers in planning and documenting children's work. The *atelierista* 'makes possible a deepening in the instruction via the use of many diverse media' (Edwards *et al*, 1993). Gandini, Hill *et al* (2005) explore how the experiences of children interacting with rich materials in the atelier affect an entire school's approach to the construction and expression of thought and learning.

From their research Cremin *et al* (2006) emphasise the significance of the enabling context in supporting playfulness, encouraging self confidence and self esteem. Adults intentionally valued children's 'agency', offering children time and space to have ideas and see these through. They stepped back, enabling children's activity to lead their support of learning.

The environment has several elements: space, including resources, allocation of time and attention (according to the Creative Foundation of Sightlines Initiative). The environment is created by the adults and is an essential part of pedagogy (the art of enabling learning). If our values include enabling creative thinking then the emotional climate must be part of the overall nurturing ethos.

> [A] Reggio school,' Bruner comments, 'is a special kind of place, one in which young human beings are invited to grow in mind, sensibility, and in belonging to a broader community ... a learning community, where mind and sensibility are shared. It is a place to learn together about the real world, and about possible worlds of the imagination. (Dahlberg *et al*, 2006).

Documentation is key to a creative learning environment to 'make the learning visible' (Giudici *et al*, 2001), as an integral tool for expression of ideas and meaning making. 'Environments where children can talk about their drawings in a serious way' (Matthews, 1999).

> Our aim is to make a school that is a place of research, learning, revisiting, reconsideration, and reflection ...

> In our approach we proceed by making plans, considering options, making cognitive reflections and symbolic representations, and refining communications skills. Active exploration and creative production by educators and children proceed without complete certainty but with a shared representation of the point of destination, the ultimate goal. (Malaguzzi in Edwards *et al*, 1998)

Carlina Rinaldi (2001) describes the process and the purpose of documentation as a 'visible trace and procedure that supports learning and teaching, making them reciprocal in that they are visible and sharable'.

> What we actually have to document is the 'emotionally moving' sense of the search for the meanings of life that children and adults undertake together ... (*ibid*)

For 5x5x5 the messages in Claxton and Carr (2002) are about the quality of the learning environment encouraged in our approach. We aimed to create a learning community in which useful resources were available, interesting projects invited children's engagement, expectations encouraged children to sustain interests over long periods, adults and children modelled and assisted each other, sharing the initiation and leadership of learning episodes.

Creative learning dispositions and schemas

Craft (2002) describes the personal attitudes and attributes of a creative disposition as 'agency; persistence; reflectiveness; openness of attitude; willingness to take risks'.

Schemas

Schemas are the universal patterns underpinning everyday behaviour. Children in their early years have a powerful drive to establish these patterns of thinking, such as understanding movements – to and fro, round and round, enveloping and containing. They achieve the development of concepts by repeating behaviours (Athey, 1990; Nutbrown, 1994). We discovered through introducing these ideas in 5x5x5 that the educators and the parents were able to encourage and support children's natural motivation to learn in this way, once they understood what was going on.

Learning dispositions

Learning dispositions is the phrase we use in 5x5x5, though they may be called habits of mind, or orientations. These attitudes or attributes are important for life-long learning, they include being willing to become involved, perseverance, resourcefulness, enquiring and being curious and sustained involvement.

Claxton and Carr (2004) draw on examples from New Zealand to illustrate the nature of the 'learning curriculum' rather than a 'content curriculum' where more attention is given to the attitudes, values and habits towards learning. The national curriculum of New Zealand, *Te Whaariki* (1996), is an example of a dispositions based approach. The framework combines five principles – empowerment, holistic development, family and community and relationships with five strands – well-being, belonging, contribution, communication and exploration.

According to Katz (1993), 'a disposition is a tendency to exhibit frequently, consciously, and voluntarily a pattern of behaviour that is directed towards a broad goal'. She gives curiosity as an example of a desirable disposition which children exhibit if they frequently respond to their environment by exploring, examining and asking questions about it.

Ferre Laevers' (2000a and b) research has demonstrated that the highest outcomes are achieved when the learning environment focuses on the well-being of children and offers them the chance for sustained involvement. He identified nine signals of involvement which colleagues in 5x5x5 found helpful in their observations: concentration, energy, complexity and creativity, facial expression and posture, persistence, precision, reaction time, language and satisfaction. 'These signals turned us around and helped us follow key children' (Kay and Angeles, 5x5x5 artist and educator).

Mention must be made of the characteristic of young children to flow from one mode of behaviour to another (Anning and Ring, 2004). These researchers adopt the word 'multi-modal' from Gunther Kress; it seems to relate strongly to the concept of the hundred languages of children. Young children shift rapidly from one form of representation to another, transforming whatever comes to hand. They show amazing flexibility of thought which we believe is a valuable capacity and indeed a creative learning disposition (see chapter 4).

The influential research work of Carol Dweck on self-perception has recently been published for the general public (2006). The essence of her theory is very relevant to 5x5x5. She shows that what counts most throughout life is the way we approach our goals, whether with a 'fixed mindset' or a 'growth mindset'. Praising children for their intelligence and ability leads them see themselves as always having to be right and successful. On the other hand a more helpful growth mindset develops when children are praised for their enquiries, efforts and problem-solving. In 5x5x5 we concentrate on processes and the creative capacity of all children, it is not about identifying children as especially talented. In rich creative climates there is no sense of failing, but of valuing all efforts.

b) UK context
Government initiatives

The four elements of creativity that we use to analyse and frame our thinking match the new set of principles of the Early Years Foundation Stage:

- A unique strong child
- Positive relationships
- Enabling environments
- Learning and development.

> The principles and philosophy of 5x5x5 resonate so strongly with those of the Early Years Foundation Stage. (Sally Jaeckle, Regional Director of the Foundation Stage, DCSF and 5x5x5=creativity Trustee)

Government and public interest in the potential of creative thinking for individuals and for the community generally is growing. The evidence from seven years of 5x5x5 research suggests that we can make a vital and effective contribution to understanding in this field. Our practice has grown in response to, and often in parallel with, national and regional policy and practice in the arts and early years education.

Our research reflects the principles of *Every Child Matters*, the Government's core policy document that now underpins all work with children nationally. 5x5x5 helps illuminate how to achieve the five *Every Child Matters* outcomes for young people:

- being healthy
- staying safe
- enjoying and achieving
- making a positive contribution
- achieving economic well-being

In 2007, the Government stressed its commitment to looking holistically at the needs of children and young people when it established the Department for Children, Schools and Families. Education and cultural policy are both moving towards creative learning. Paul Roberts' report (2006) called for the recognition of enrichment learning:

> Creativity is not at odds with raising standards ... in order for it to flourish we need to ensure that it is embedded in our developing education policies and not a bolt on set of activities ... Creativity enriches young people's lives in school, beyond the school day and through informal learning and leisure activities. It develops critical thinking and problem solving skills which can be applied across the curriculum and it promotes artistic development and appreciation.

There is much debate about whether the prescribed curriculum has narrowed to a point where many of our young people are launching into adult life lacking the flexible creative thinking required for negotiating a complex world. We need to provide opportunities for creative learning for young people and for professional development in creative learning for educators. Teachers are calling for 'permission to take risks', to finally take ownership of their own creative role, to be involved with research and learning themselves to enable young people to take charge of their own learning. As adults, teachers are 'companions' in research and learning, helping young people to ask good questions for exploration, providing feedback, reflection and support.

A *Curriculum Innovation Survey* in 2006 led by HMI identified key characteristics of curriculum innovation which match 5x5x5 principles:

- Role play, drama, art, music contributes significantly
- Pupils carry out substantial research
- Adults and children work together in project or problem-solving teams
- Pupils make real choices and mentor each other
- Original and ground-breaking non-traditional curricula
- Flexible time periods
- Local environment used very creatively

Above all, these schools engage their pupils in an open-ended investigative approach to learning in which pupils' interest is engaged, where there is a sense of purpose and relevance, where pupils are active participants and where learning is fun. (Mick Waters Director of Curriculum, QCA, 2006)

5x5x5=creativity is built on principles of participation and democracy. It values individual motivation and supports personal choice and control in lifelong learning. The greater the investment in individual creativity, in families, schools and cultural organisations, the more likely we are to build sustainable, vibrant communities.

c) The wider context

'Creativity is a process of seeing new possibilities'. (Robinson, 2001)

Standing alongside our work, we have been impressed by other initiatives that place learning at the heart of any 'curriculum'. These also prioritise a process led curriculum based on generic skills and capacities.

The Royal Society of Arts *Opening Minds* project suggests a family of *learning competences*: learning, managing information, relating to people, managing situations and citizenship:

- understanding how to learn, taking account of one's preferred learning styles, and understanding the need to, and how to, manage one's own learning throughout life

- learning, systematically, to think

- exploring and reaching an understanding of one's own creative talents, and how to make best use of them

- learning to enjoy and love learning for its own sake and as part of understanding oneself

- achieving high standards in literacy, numeracy, and spatial understanding

- achieving high standards of competence in handling information and communication technology and understanding the underlying processes.

Schools in this project have cut down the subject curriculum in order to develop a competency/skills driven curriculum, giving empowerment to students supported by a teacher/mentor. Results already show dramatic improvements in motivation, behaviour, people skills and communication skills for both students and staff. This work is now moving into a Future Schools Network, considering implications for future organisations.

Project Zero's mission is to understand and enhance learning, thinking, and creativity in the arts, as well as in humanistic and scientific disciplines, at individual and institutional levels. Colleagues at *Project Zero*, Harvard (Giudici *et al*, 2001), have identified four essential questions to guide their work. The first three questions articulate overarching themes for our work; the fourth question addresses our goal of making this work more accessible to educators in general.

Individual and group learning: How do learning groups form, function, and demonstrate understanding?

Documentation: How can documentation support, extend, and make visible individual and group learning (and deepen our understandings about teaching and learning more broadly)?

Culture, values, and democracy: How does this work help us to understand and address issues of equity and diversity in relation to individual and group learning in our classrooms and schools?

Dissemination: How can we help each other and other educators enter into this work?

Project Zero's Thinking Classroom is all about the teaching of critical and creative thinking to help educators attend to:

- the dispositional side of student thinking and learning
- transfer of student knowledge to new contexts
- assessment of specific thinking performances
- identification of rich thinking opportunities in the regular curriculum

The *artful thinking palette* is comprised of 6 thinking dispositions which emphasise intellectual behaviours: questioning and investigating, observing and describing, exploring multiple viewpoints, reasoning with evidence, finding complexity, comparing and connecting. (http://www.pz.harvard.edu/Research/ArtThink.htm)

Similarly, the *New Basics Curriculum* in Queensland is completed by an organisational 'triad' of Productive Pedagogies (20 teaching repertoires) and Rich Tasks (suites of assessed tasks that are intellectually challenging, relate to real-world skills and completed over 3 years). The pedagogies are based on: recognition of difference, connectedness, intellectual quality and a supportive classroom environment. Each *New Basics* cluster is designed to help pupils answer a critical question:

Who am I and where am I going? How do I make sense of and communicate with the world? What are my rights and responsibilities in communities, cultures and economies? How do I describe, analyse and shape the world around me?

The *New Basics* are predicated on the existence of mindful schools, where intellectual engagement and connectedness to the real world are constant foci.

These ideas of modularisation, of learner independence, relevant, meaningful and constructivist experiences seem to have been organised together in a structure for learning in schools, which makes eminent sense. It also has clear theoretical underpinnings drawn from the work of John Dewey, Lev Vygotsky, Paulo Freire and Ted Sizer.

What is common to these creative curricula is emphasis on a thematic approach to teaching and learning designed to support children's natural curiosity and stimulate their creativity. If direct experience is placed at the centre, children's thinking and creative capacities can be supported in a meaningful context. Within a creative environment, children, adults and parents can work with each other in depth to develop their sense of responsibility in companionship.

Conclusion

This chapter has shown that the principles and work of 5x5x5 resonate with current research and government aspirations. There is a new will to listen to children and ensure that their education is compatible with their dispositions, modes of thinking and expression. This makes sense in the culture of the world in which they are growing up.

> You cannot legislate for people's understanding ... but rather the adoption of a process of questioning, dialogue, reflection and meaning making ... it is work continually in progress. (Dahlberg *et al*, 1999)

It is clear that we need more opportunities for 'sustained shared thinking', to support and challenge children's thinking by getting involved in the thinking process with them. We want children to have original and unexpected ideas, to speculate about possibilities that are purposeful, imaginative and creative. Above all we want children to keep their minds wide open, to be curious, playful and take risks in a safe environment.

3

Making 5x5x5=creativity work:
the invisible framework

a) The role of documentation
Andrea Sully

The power within simple ideas

'All that we need to know about children for children is best learnt from children themselves' (Malaguzzi in Edwards *et al*, 1998). This simple yet potentially powerful idea is an important place to begin in our understanding of 'documentation' and how to develop it within our own practice. Malaguzzi goes on:

> Stand aside for a while and leave room for learning, observe carefully what children do, and then, if you have understood well, perhaps teaching will be different from before.

Accepting the basic simplicity of this idea is the first step in discovering that genuinely tuning in to children's thoughts and ideas is a more complex process than we might have imagined. The difference for us, as adults looking in on childhood, lies in the relative range of experiences children have to draw upon to make sense of their world. Though their frame of reference is smaller than ours, this does not belie their capacity to enquire, problem solve, reason and think creatively.

Once we acknowledge that children are competent thinkers we will need to take an imaginative step into their world, to explore with them the meaning of their logic. This leads us towards a much more complex interpretation of their learning experiences. Standing back, listening, and seeing what children offer us in their thoughts and actions, will require us to consider something else, the consequences of our own emotional and logical engagement, interpretation and choices.

Subjectivity in learning and teaching

We cannot experience anything without making it our own. Our personality, emotions and acts of mind will necessarily shape our interpretation. Observation can only be a subjective process because we cannot distinguish between the sensory information we gather and the interpretation that we bring to it. Here is a wonderfully liberating thought for the world of education: 'Maintain a readiness to change points of view so as never to have too many certainties' (*ibid*).

Documentation places before us possibilities for personal and professional reflection that could provide a catalyst for change – celebrating the craft-knowledge or art of teaching. It is liberating: we cannot be 'wrong' in how we do it nor in our own reflections. But at the same time we need to accept that we may not be absolutely accurate about our interpretations of what we have seen and heard.

This is how all research develops and documentation can become a research tool for educators. Interpretations of children's thinking develop into hypotheses and we find ourselves 'researching children researching the world.'

When we document children's learning and try to offer our own thoughts about what is happening, we are engaged in 'research in practice'. In Reggio, documenting is the linchpin of continuing professional development, done with colleagues. New understandings are forged through this researchful practice and practitioners become increasingly confident and articulate.

The role of the adult in places of learning

Young children's flexibility of thought and ideas seems to lead us towards something that our education system may not yet be prepared for. Learning is subjective, complex and cannot be mandated and needs us to reinterpret our role becoming 'researchers in practice' rather than all-knowing teachers.

Our role in this context is to draw out the thoughts and ideas of children and to support their learning once we have first established what matters to them. Similarly, we can see just how much children seek out teachers themselves to support and lead them in their learning.

Documentation is deliciously unpredictable. It also becomes multi-layered and challenging because it must reflect the unique, rich and abstract nature of every child's mind. The child is constantly acting upon the world with their drive to make sense, form connections, and develop their understanding. This requires us to acknowledge that we need to make choices about the best ways and contexts to develop, nurture and support children's lines of enquiry, with no guarantees that we have got it right.

So documenting the active learning that engages children's hearts and minds begins to mirror the complexity of learning itself. Documenting is a tool that helps make the learning process visible but also makes evident the unpredictability and complexity of the processes we traditionally think of as teaching and learning.

Curious children require curious adults

Documentation as an approach requires adults to be just as curious as children in 'researching children, researching the world'. If we believe in listening as a pedagogical tool, then it is worth considering why this is important. It seems that the key behaviour we are demonstrating to children is one of attention when we listen. Nancy Kline (1998) points out that it is the quality of our attention that will help determine the quality of people's thinking. When listening is of a high calibre, the human mind cannot help but be ignited. In Reggio, this listening approach leads to the development of experiences that challenge and further provoke children's thinking. Teachers write a 'declaration of intent' rather than prescriptive forward planning. This is described by practitioners in Reggio Emilia as a 'listening pedagogy'.

Documentation enables and requires the practitioner to take responsibility for understanding the process of children's thinking, not from a book or national initiative, but from the very children in front of them, with whom they share their time. Documentation in this sense becomes the most powerful and effective professional development tool available to us.

Documentation as an approach

Documentation is an approach to learning and teaching that is like no other. To document, it would seem, is to ascribe to every child their own place in the sun. It is a constructivist approach, rooted in the belief that learning is about the space between what we understand now and what we do not yet understand. The most favourable context for bridging this space is to be amongst others, for learning is an innately social process.

29

The importance of relationships

The quality of the learning relationships is the key to effective documentation. The power of children to learn from each other is often underestimated and we may, as a result, miss powerful opportunities to allow learning to flourish. When we document what children say and do, we begin to value the way they learn from each other, recognising personal preferences, fields of expertise, knowledge bases, interests and schemas.

This leads us to consider the responsibility we are offering children in their own learning and the extent to which we both expect and enable them to use their own minds; to make choices; ask their own questions; construct their own meanings; understand their rights and responsibilities as active citizens in the school community.

Nothing ventured, nothing gained

Through documenting we become more tuned in to children, more skilled at analysing and interpreting their actions and projecting possibilities for further enquiry. The uncertainty of it all is what makes it a dynamic learning approach for the teacher just as much as it does for the children. It rewards us in developing our own sense of agency as professional educators. Unlike many of our professional edicts and experiences, there is nothing prescriptive about documenting.

Documenting children's learning also challenges the traditional 'transmission model' of learning because it reveals the uncertainties in our own thinking about learning. It requires us to reflect about what we have observed and project what might be going on inside the minds of the children. In this way, it validates confusion and doubt as learning opportunities for both adults and children. Carlina Rinaldi (2006) reminds us of the value of moving away from seeing doubt, confusion and error as moments of weakness to seeing them as rich learning opportunities. Learning itself can then be upheld, as subjective, dynamic, and constructed within the companionship of others.

Open-eyed playfulness

Children never fail to surprise us in their own interpretations of the world, which so often have within them a logic of childhood that is more endearing or sensible than reality itself. This is important as it is one of the factors that make documentation professionally fulfilling. The children's interpretations of the world offer us once again the world through the eyes of a child, open to new possibilities, novelty and playful ideas. The playfulness with ideas that characterises children's thinking can become quite contagious. The warmth and closeness of relationships between both children and adults that follows the process of documentation can bring increased humour to the setting. This way of working nourishes the adults as much as it does the children.

Partnership in learning

When teachers and educators have faith in children's capacities and use documentation as part of everyday teaching, planning becomes acutely tuned to what the children think and understand and therefore where they might go next. Documentation is arguably a model of formative assessment at its most sophisticated and best. It supports the principles and strengthens the current national focus on assessment for learning. Prior knowledge will always be noted and children involved in self-evaluation. Observation and reflection will be used as teaching tools, questioning will be related to genuine enquiry, children will be firmly at the heart of the process and assessment will sustain our planning.

Documentation also challenges the unsatisfactory interpretation of learning as a passive process that is linear and cumulative. Documentation, in contrast, promotes the idea of a partnership in the teaching and learning relationships in which the child has an equal opportunity to ask the questions, seek the answers, generate ideas and delight with adults in the uncertainties of human knowledge and experience. The partnership approach is compatible with the ethos of *Every Child Matters*, which requires children to be listened to in respect of their learning and fully engaged in the development of the curriculum. Documentation thus strengthens children's entitlement to greater levels of freedom and creativity.

Making choices and taking risks

Documentation entails taking professional risks and making choices to affirm our commitment to protecting children's rights to learning experiences that are both empowering and meaningful. It needs us to be strong, competent and skilful in supporting children's thinking and planning their next steps. It can be a transformational tool in deepening our own practice through opportunities for reflection and dialogue. In this way, documentation simultaneously scaffolds both the adults' and the children's learning, a process through which our own potential as teachers and educators can be advanced.

Presenting learning through documentation

We need to re-consider the current practise of displaying children's work in many schools and settings. Typically this involves either a teaching display with prompts and reminders for learning or a display of children's work (often perceived to be the best pieces of work), sometimes annotated with notes about the context. This could constitute display in Reggio terms, but often lacks informed adult reflection and analysis of the children's thinking, and projection about the future possibilities for their learning. Very seldom do teachers consider displaying the work that was not fully understood or went wrong for a child, or a product that was not completed satisfactorily.

Starting small

The move from display to documentation can be started in a small way. Short cameos of children in either group scenarios or alone can be presented as learning stories. This is followed by reflection related to resources, the environment and practical activities. One cannot help but generate questions from these close observations. Why do the children discard the plastic plates? What would happen if we used real china, glass or real vegetables? Why do the boys use the sand more than the girls? Why do we stop the children exploring the physical attributes of a big puddle? When a setting starts to document it becomes a very effective, relevant and personalised self-evaluation tool because it will generate questions about us. It acts as both a mirror and lens for the school or setting.

Practically speaking

Using photographs, children's drawings, their words, video, and learning stories are all useful remembering and re-visiting tools. They enable both adults and children to look back at a previous moment, reconsider the significance of the experience and reconstruct their meanings. The notion of rapidly changing displays can also be re-assessed if they are replaced with learning stories that are constantly revisited by the children and added to when appropriate. Many children are adept at recalling from visual cues as they tend to have an eidetic memory (visual) and unlike adults can often remember which children were not even in the photographs!

Documentation panels can also be used to support transition and continuity for children as old panels can be moved into a new classroom. Children feel connected with their past and with the sense of the shared experiences and community of the class.

Children as allies

Documenting will also give young children a strong message about their value. They quickly come to appreciate that what they have to say and offer is truly valued as these are kept as mementos of their life in the setting. The following are some thoughts from children ages 3-4 years during 5x5x5 work with an artist when asked why we documented.

> To show everyone what we does do (Tommy).
>
> Cause we like putting our pictures on the wall.
>
> Who looks at it (adult)?
>
> Teachers, kids, mummies and daddies (Katie).
>
> The photos show us what we are doing (Callum).
>
> So it doesn't get lost.
>
> What doesn't get lost (adult)?
>
> The pictures of the children, they is learning (Kayleigh).
>
> So we can remember (Liam).

These visual and written records of learning also become ways to communicate to others the ethos and approach of the school or setting. Documentation can be displayed on panels of card (and if laminated displayed on the outside of the setting too for the community to see) and kept later in large art folders as an archive. This may be helpful when outside agencies visit or in sharing with families. More importantly, they can repeatedly be used with children. One cohort of children may well share a similar interest or point of fascination to that of previous children. If this is the case, the panels can become a great source of delight. Most children are fascinated by the work of other children. It offers children different perspectives and ideas which provoke new thinking while creating a sense of history.

In dialogue with parents

Documentation should be shared regularly with parents: documentation provides a forum for seeking parents' expert thoughts on their own children and testing our hypotheses. Parents of children who are not featured that week, month or term still see that when so much care is taken over other children, their own child is constantly valued in the setting.

Families can offer us a different perspective, which further adds to the complexity of documenting and its richness of interpretation. Parents deeply value the opportunity to share in their child's learning journey. Documentation can also support the relationship building between child and family, as a new perspective on a child is offered back to the parents from the setting (see case study of John on page 96).

Sharing our pedagogy and thoughts with parents in these ways goes much further than just involving them. It is participation exemplifying the principles of listening, relationships and community.

To conclude

Carlina Rinaldi rightly describes children as 'the greatest listeners' to the world about them; they often enable us to enrich our own thinking and in turn our professional lives. We surely owe it to them to make visible what they have to say, and act as the guardians of a long and supported childhood. In doing so we may not just be making learning visible but also the treasures of childhood itself.

Documenting as an approach will undoubtedly offer us nourishment and strength in our everyday professional lives and as Vea Vecchi sums it all up, it is 'a unique source of knowledge ... it is precious material for teachers, but also for the children, for the family and whoever wishes to get closer to the strategies in children's ways of thinking.'

A version of this article appeared in ReFocus Journal *No.3 Summer 2006.*

Professional development session on the role and responsibility of documentation
Ed Harker

Introduction
When does recording become documentation? We are all familiar with recording in our own lives such as diaries, phones, photos, notes, sketches. But when do these involve the shared reflection which is at the heart of documentation?

Discussion groups
Colleagues worked in small groups to define 'documentation'. All the suggestions were combined to create: 'An organic, growing, subjective, investigative story of journeys with commentary, both written and visual; a multi-media tool with interpretation and different perspectives coming together and being made visible, to make meaning and that captures key learning moments, and that is an aide memoire, and re-presentation!'

Project Zero (http://www.pz.harvard.edu/mlv) describes documentation as visible listening and suggests five features:

■   A question guides the observations, often focussed on ways of learning

■   There is collective analysis, strengthened by multiple perspectives

■   There are many ways to represent the experience observed, multiple languages (a variety of media: written, diagrammatic, images etc.)

■   Documentation needs to be shared, it is not private. It becomes public as it is shared with all learners: children, parents or teachers

■   It can inform future plans.

From the discussions feedback included:
1. A question guides the observations, often focused on ways of learning
The research question at the back of your mind influences what you notice. Several different views can give a more rounded view.

2. There is collective analysis
Parent documentation can be problematic if notes are handed in to the reflective team (artist, teacher and cultural centre). If the parents are not part of reflection, there is no explanation of their documentation. Even so the notes can stimulate recall as a narrative journal. Best practice is to share and reflect on documentation together as group. Finding enough time for reflective discussion can be difficult.

Mia
It's Sunny.

Sadie:
It has not got
any leaves on

Holly
It's winter.
Sadie
The Start of
The year.

Katie - It must be
...the Toothlit
walk cos trees have
no roof on!

Millie
-When it
rained it
poured down.
It's dark

Jenna
No, I think
it's just
in flattime.

Jonah
Then why
are we
at school?

Holly - maybe it's the Torchlit Walk!

Documentation from St Saviour's Nursery and Infant School

3. There are many ways to represent the experience observed
Challenge of keeping documentation fresh. Colleagues could experiment using sound-recording and other technologies (see Creative Digital Technologies section).

4. Documentation needs to be shared with learners
Documentation is for sharing. Methods used need to be effective, they must be open, visible, and understandable.

Everyone in the project is a learner.

The layers of documentation reach children, educators, artists, cultural centres, parents and the wider community.

Central to documentation is the question: who are you presenting to and why?

It is important to highlight points you want to make visible to a particular group.

Sharing documentation with children needs to be immediate, though conversely Ed described children reflecting in detail on photographs several months after the event.

Artists are making learning visible and accessible, they are helping to make learning apparent outside the curriculum.

A key function of artists in Reggio Emilia is making layers accessible at all times; a creative way of sharing experience through art.

There are different readings of the events by artists and educators, these different understandings add to the parent's knowledge of their child. We should hold on to differences and not dilute them – multi-dimensional documentation is the most valuable.

Essence of artwork is a provocation for reflection allowing a broader representation.

Documentation allows possibilities in interpretation, it does not shut down alternative ideas. Documentation as a process: can change depending on what you connect with in the dynamic experience. Documentation as a meeting place: if one thing moves, everything moves. It can be a place where paths cross, it is not fixed. 'Nothing gets under a parent's skin more quickly and more permanently than the illumination of his or her own child's behaviour' (Athey, 1990).

b) Creative and reflective cycle
Susi Bancroft and Mary Fawcett

Active engagement in a creative and reflective cycle is part of the 'invisible structure' which makes 5x5x5 work. The case studies in chapter 4 tell the stories of three triangles using the cycle. This section will explain the underlying structure and the processes involved. At the first professional development for 5x5x5, colleagues from Sightlines Initiative suggested models from the Creative Foundation project.

Some triangles have developed their own individual pattern of reflection. At the heart of the process is the continuous cycle of hypothesising, experimenting, reflecting and hypothesising again. Each step is explained below in simple terms.

Getting started
For all colleagues, artists, educators and cultural centres, starting out in 5x5x5 research for the first time can seem daunting. Many educational approaches expect the adults to plan initiatives, while 5x5x5 expects the balance to shift towards the children taking responsibility, in other words, working with child-initiated interests. Not only does the openness seem risky, it may seem very puzzling to some people until they come to understand the whole philosophical concept.

Observation
Time is spent in establishing adult relationships and then, in the setting, the artist will spend several sessions with the class or group of children, taking time to get to know them, talk to them and notice their interests. Regularly in the end of year evaluation interviews, participants comment on how these sensitive observation times are crucial to later success. The artist is also able to establish some familiarity with the settings, people, routines and resources.

Review time
Artist, educator and possibly mentor sit down together to share their observations and perceptions of the session. Both artist and educator have different perspectives and identify some of the current fascinations of the children and some priorities of their own. Educators often talk of the value of the artist observations, offering a fresh view or developing a 'third eye'. Together the adults will be beginning the process of identifying key elements and aspects of the children's thinking.

Hypothesising

In Reggio Emilia they talk of *progettazione* – projecting forward possible themes and actions – an idea rather different from our word 'project' which is much more defined. At this stage in 5x5x5 colleagues begin to suggest possible flexible directions and what they might need to prepare, do or what resources to acquire for these. Usually this is the moment to agree an initial provocation. As far as possible this is a democratic triangle decision.

The provocation

A provocation will take different forms. It may provide a resource or a material for children to experiment with or it may be about engaging with an experience offered as a stimulus. Among the favourite provocations is a walk in the vicinity of the setting, a visit to the cultural centre or another place of interest. Usually the whole class will make the expedition, supported by helpers and parents and everyone will be charged to listen attentively and to observe children's spontaneous interests.

A walk typically reveals enthusiasms for found objects such as sticks, mud, streams, stones and leaves drawn from the experience of being outdoors with natural elements. On one memorable walk in nearby Freshford, the children were imaginatively fired, convinced there were bears living in a wooded area.

Review of the provocation

Everyone's notes and comments are brought together and a picture slowly emerges of different approaches among the children. One mentor commented that some children saw the environment as 'historians' asking 'Did the Romans come here?' At St Saviour's children adopted a scientific style of exploration: collecting, prodding mud with sticks to understand its texture and properties. Some were builders, wanting to construct with sticks and yet others were the storytellers, imaginatively creating worlds of monsters. Children can move fluidly and rapidly between these approaches.

How to identify lasting themes which will be shared by a number of children can be challenging and cannot be forecast with certainty. This adds to the fascination though, and adults try to keep in mind an openness to possible changes of direction. There is self reflection on both the provision of experience for the children and on personal engagement with the collaboration.

Planning the first session

Much will depend on how many children are to be involved and also what kind of media is used to start with. In some classes everyone will have access to resources. For example the construction and mark-making possibilities offered by the artists will be available alongside the free choice materials of the class. Sometimes smaller groups are taken in turn to a separate space with the artist, educator and documenter: the school hall, spare classroom or part of the outside area may be used. At St Stephen's the 'quiet garden' has been the location this year.

Analysis of first session

What actually happened? What learning dispositions were shown – curiosity, willingness to be involved, concentration? What kinds of explorations were observed? Were there surprises? Which children were working together? What ideas were emerging? What was capturing their imaginations? Were any particular schemas in evidence? How did the documenters manage? How well did adults collaborate? And so on, with plenty of interesting questions and sharing of perspectives. From this the outline of the next session is planned and prepared.

The regular pattern of creative planning and reflection

Analysis or review sessions follow after each visit of the artist, or trip.

Everyone – artist, educator, mentor, cultural centre colleague, parent documenter – whoever has been present, has a voice in the discussion. The episodes are re-visited and re-interpreted. The subjectivity of any observer is recognised and valued. Informal brief exchanges may also take place by phone or email.

A written and visual record is kept. This gives a brief description of the activity, which children were most involved, what possibilities were opening up and how to prepare for these – who is to be responsible for what. These are informal notes designed to be shared and useful – to make learning visible and there for discussion (see the case study of St Saviour's and the section on documentation for examples).

Issues

There are similarities in this style of working with other reflective teaching models. One example would be *High Scope*, with its format of 'Plan Do Review'. Another example would be the action research cycle used by some artists and some educators for practical research. Our particular model has now become an established part of being involved in 5x5x5.

From our experience of 5x5x5 in many schools, we know that to implement the creative reflective cycle requires considerable commitment and negotiation. Supply cover might be needed in order to release teachers or teaching assistants. These decisions may be challenging for schools and settings to negotiate. However from our evaluations we know that where reflection sessions are valued and given adequate time, then the benefits and depth of the effects of this kind of reflective research have considerable impact.

Choosing the best time for the reflection sessions is another issue. Some headteachers may prefer not to commit staff to attend after school meetings. In practice we have observed that there are many ingenious ways of solving these challenges. Solutions are usually found when there are strong collaborative relationships and clear support for each other as well as the generation of excitement about the research process. The collaborative learning and multi-disciplinary nature of the process is refreshing and thought-provoking. Longer-term research periods also help embed the approach in the setting. The generosity of spirit and goodwill from whole staff teams make the creative reflective cycle a reality.

Once established as routine these sessions are remarkably creative and enjoyable. After 5.00 pm on a long day with an early start, one teacher exclaimed: 'I am enjoying this!'

Writing of comparable experience in USA Barbara Burrington writes:

> We have discovered a cycle of enquiry that constantly re-emerges: an encounter between children and materials coincides with their imagination or interest, is recorded by the teacher or saved in an artefact, and is retold by children and teachers, which becomes a provocation to pursue the encounter into the future. It is a continuous cycle of perching and flying. Like birds landing and taking off, children and teachers survey the terrain and ascend in order to gain a new perspective. (in Gandini *et al*, 2005)

c) Collaboration and partnership
Susi Bancroft and Mary Fawcett

> Our most important and valuable ideas are products of shared enthusiasms and ambitions learned in the joy and hurt of companionship. (Trevarthen, 2006)

Reciprocity is in the spirit of 5x5x5 research. There is a flow of giving and taking, sharing mutual interest and respect, a flow between artist, educator and children. Where this works well there is a seamlessness – roles are merged. It is a treasured concept where research begins with personal reflection supported, extended and enriched through collaboration.

Democracy and equality are implicit in this community of learners. Where it works well it is truly a partnership.

The framework
The structure of 5x5x5 was consciously framed as a triangle: artist, educator and cultural centre, working creatively with children and each other. This structure aims for creative encounters full of challenging possibilities which happen through the bringing together of adults from different perspectives. The potential lies in the exciting and unique dynamic of the triangle which is supported by a mentor.

The wider community also comes together into groupings and other partnerships in various ways:

- small local authority groups
- the whole research group
- mentors
- evaluators
- artists and cultural centres
- AND (artist network development group)
- 5x5x5 Board of Trustees

Within the setting parents are welcome partners and the whole setting is invited to be a part of the research. Increasingly as 5x5x5 develops over time other age groups, such as secondary school students and adults, are drawn in to the process.

The structure has a specific intention – to challenge the equilibrium of all with the goal of nurturing everyone's creative capacities. The drawing together of colleagues from different disciplines will naturally lead to challenging assumptions and asking questions about each other's practice. For this to be a positive experience, relationships need to be consciously built, supported and maintained.

The philosophy
The spirit of 5x5x5 is about learning in collaborative partnership. When collaborations are truly about reciprocity then, as one educator says, 'it is wonderful to be doubtful.' Working together supports the individual so that enquiry can be deeper and more challenging as each draws on collective experience.

The educational principle is that we learn more deeply and effectively through reflection, exchange and dialogue with others. When we combine knowledge, ask questions of each other, demand explanations, hypotheses and theories from ourselves, then new knowledge is discovered, wider connections are made and fresh meanings are created to share. This principle relates to the kind of scaffolding for children – sustained shared thinking – deemed to be most productive for learning and cognitive development by *REPEY* (Siraj-Blatchford *et al*, 2002).

5x5x5 goes wider and deeper than most initiatives in schools and settings since the approach actively invites the individual to be a questioning researcher rather than to be confined by a prescribed curriculum. It follows action research as defined by McNiff and Whitehead (2002) where research is 'genuinely about personal and collective relationships'. As 5x5x5 states: we are researching ourselves researching children researching the world. Theories emerging from 5x5x5 are actively grounded in practice when engaging in research together.

The philosophy of collaboration requires cultural learning, it is about companionship in learning and will 'add to the community's story of knowledge and skill, to the imagining and style of its art and to the joy of participation' (Trevarthen, 2006).

Shared language
Reflective practitioners from different professional fields working together need an underpinning structure if the possibilities of the collaboration are to be effectively realised. Relationships are at the centre of success. Time and attention needs to be consciously invested from the beginning in order to develop a sound rapport and a working language.

For the adults involved, democracy is promoted. Equality of professional roles needs to be established. Real empathy, sharing and listening, truly receiving each other – these are not idealistic words or empty rhetoric but the proven basis for creative work to have lasting impact.

From their professional training and experience each person brings a language and taken-for-granted meanings. In the context of 5x5x5 a shared language has to be found and established. New metaphors need to be created before we can work together to develop deeper meanings and learning which all understand and are part of.

This is a challenge since our research is based in educational settings. These organisations have an established and sometimes exclusive language. Nevertheless so does the art world itself. Indeed one artist speaks of her need to talk in her 'mother tongue'. Committed exploration and a genuine desire to learn each other's language is therefore essential.

New expressions of language are encouraged especially as artists from many art forms are involved. This supports Rinaldi's assertion of a new culture where reflection and discourse on learning happen with 'enrichment that derives from the integrated and interconnected use of multiple languages' (Rinaldi, 2001).

Parents

For parents 5x5x5 offers a real opportunity to understand children's creative thinking and expression and to support its development in schools. 5x5x5 research originates from children's own interests, fascinations and thinking.

It offers parents a rare and vital chance to understand and value their own children.

Opportunities for learning more about 5x5x5 come through presentation and discussion, the exhibitions, participation in documenting experiences. Chapter 5 includes one parent's presentation on the experience of documenting and other parents' expressions of their experiences.

A new culture

5x5x5 aims to develop a new culture where creativity is valued and central to both education and our culture.

> To be encouraged to think for yourself, in the company of other thinkers, to ask difficult and searching questions about your practice and provision, to learn to think more critically and reflectively, as the educators in 5x5x5 have been doing, could be the beginning of a radically different culture in the early years ... (Drummond, 2005)

(d) The role of the mentor in 5x5x5=creativity
Mary Fawcett and Penny Hay

What is a mentor?

There are over 100 definitions of a mentor. We hear about mentors working with young people where an experienced respected person supports the younger and inexperienced. The term may be applied to a supervisor, a guru or expert, a counsellor or an adviser. Tutor or teacher might describe the relationship better. What does a mentor actually do in his or her face-to-face meetings with the mentee? The role is difficult to explain as it is so variable. Relationships, perceptions of power, imparting knowledge, encouraging reflection, supporting colleagues in challenging situations are all part of the mentoring role.

> A mentor can be described as a questioning person, probing (not inquisitor), perhaps a research-full friend, trusted, expected and expecting to ask people to reflect on what they've done ... to get them to analyse. (Mary Fawcett)

The emergence of the role of mentor in 5x5x5

In the early days of 5x5x5 when there were just five early years settings working with their artists and cultural centres, all in Bath and North East Somerset, maintaining communication was relatively easy. During the first year we discovered that a 'creative learning community' (as identified by Tamsyn Imison) was vital in sustaining the adults in their role as educators and artists in collaborative relationships and in building physical and psychological creative environments.

The role of mentor has developed as the project has grown. The co-ordinator (now Director of Research), as a part-time researcher, could not physically maintain the degree of contact necessary with each triangle when larger numbers were involved. The mentors originally met on a regular basis as a 'kitchen table group' – the KTG started meeting around Penny's kitchen table! A team of mentors now respond to the specific needs of the triangle members, the artist, the educators, colleagues in the cultural centres. The research is now punctuated with regular meetings to give an overview of progress as well as to raise issues that will benefit from the support of the group.

Values and principles of mentoring in 5x5x5

Sometimes we talk about 5x5x5 having an 'invisible framework', supporting changing educational practice. Every setting has a mentor who maintains regular supportive contact throughout the project. This person may be a member of the research team, a local authority adviser or consultant, a lecturer at Bath Spa University, an experienced artist or educator. The mentors respond to the specific needs of the triangle members, the artist, the educators and colleagues in the cultural centres. They are ambassadors for the principles of the research and will have a wider understanding of the possibilities of working in this way than new colleagues joining the project.

The circumstances and context of mentoring are significant. The overall project and the individual partnerships can be so varied that the word mentor cannot be used in a generalised all-purpose way. Through the years the role has developed in response to the changing needs of the project and the participants.

In common with Reggio Emilia, 5x5x5 has developed a culture of research and enquiry at all levels. A key to the quality of Reggio practice may well be the full involvement of artists in the educational process together with the role of the *pedagogista*. While the *pedagogista* has some relationship to that of the 5x5x5 mentor, it is closer to that of our local authority advisers (see Filippini in Edwards *et al*, 1998).

5x5x5=creativity principles (see chapter 1) form the basis of our approach. Each one of these principles, though referring to working with children, is in fact closely related to the actual role of the mentor in 5x5x5 working with the adults.

Respectful relationships: these are not hierarchical relationships, where the mentor is the superior holder of knowledge initiating people into a secret garden. It is important that the mentor respect the strengths and competences of their mentees. The process should feel participatory and democratic, not one of instruction and direction. In her work with children, one educator speaks of being 'beside the children.' Similarly mentors are in a partnering role.

Co-construction of knowledge: the adults are all researchers who are together constructing their roles and a body of knowledge in the frame of mentoring. The mentor, as is the case with the artist or educator in relation to the children, may know more than the children about certain things and have more experience, but their role is as participant in a shared enquiry.

Following the smoke: in the case of mentoring in 5x5x5, there is no prescribed body of knowledge, no curriculum or blue-print, which incidentally makes it easier to be open and inquisitive. On the other hand it can also feel risky and uncertain. The mentor is not a guru.

Creative reflective cycle: this is a very appropriate model for the process of mentoring. The pattern of observation, hypothesising, engagement, reflection, further planning is comparable. Specifically, to challenge and provoke questions which enable the researchers to go beyond the everyday and to look into the emerging themes behind the particular contexts.

Mentor as facilitator and enabler: The mentor is not there in the role of instructor or assessor. One of the most important strategies is enabling the mentee to ask questions, to interrogate their own practice, questions such as 'What questions do you have?' 'What choices can you make?' It is hoped that they can learn through the reality of their own experiences. As with children, the type of questions and the way in which they are asked is critical. Where this is done sensitively it can enrich practice. One educator said 'We would like a small M in our pocket all the time to help us ask good questions'.

The comparison of adults with children and mentors with mentees can only be taken so far. There are major differences and one mentor claimed the mentor role was much harder than working with children. Power relationships between adults and children, the developmental stages of children and the responsibilities of the adults are among the key differences.

The role should not be underestimated. As Filippini says, 'the art of working with other adults – be they teachers or colleagues – demands a long apprenticeship' (*ibid*).

The realities of mentoring

The actual work falls broadly into two parts – notably face-to-face sessions with colleagues in the setting, and review meetings or professional development with other mentors. Mentors support their triangles flexibly, according to need and opportunity. The range of visits include preparation, reviews, work sessions, documentation and reflection meetings. There are also many informal contacts to support both the practicalities and reflective processes.

Mentors support the evaluation process too. Before the work with the children begins, observations of the setting plus an evaluation interview with the educator are carried out by the mentor. Towards completion of the period of the artist's engagement with the children they conduct a second interview. Mentors have time allocated over the year during which they will make regular visits to the settings while the artist is there; they engage with the cultural centre and take part in some of the reflection sessions. During the preparation of exhibitions and seminars the mentor has a key part in helping artists and educators in the selection and presentation of the children's learning stories.

Away from the setting the mentors also attend professional development sessions for mentors, organised by Bath Spa University. For some this is leading to a Masters qualification through a specially designed module. There are regular review meetings with other mentors in their own local authority group and across the whole 5x5x5 project. The mentors meet about six times over the year.

The professional development and review sessions allow the participating adults to build and foster a shared set of values, develop trusting relationships, find a shared language for discussing their observations and interpretations, to examine challenging situations and to discover alternative ways of dealing with them.

The role of the mentor might seem straightforward and uncontroversial, but the approach of 5x5x5 is about bringing change in educational and creative practice. Katz (1994) discusses the challenge of change, especially in connection with the ideas from Reggio Emilia as they relate to practice in USA. In the UK Mary Jane Drummond talks about being brave in taking risks, as for example in starting from the fascinations and hypotheses of the children (2005). Relying on observations of children and planning in an open-ended, responsive way that contrasts with the tightly structured timetable feels unpredictable, like sailing in uncharted waters.

Mentors have other roles too. They may help colleagues improve their skills as documenters, perhaps by modelling this research technique. Once the adults have gathered written records and images, the mentors, with their breadth of experience, again contribute suggestions about ways of selecting, creating information for parents, colleagues and the children (see documentation in this chapter). Mentors are also involved in the meetings for parents and other staff in the school or setting to discuss the underpinning principles and the practice of 5x5x5.

Finally, mentors frequently have to explain and support the selection of a focus group within a large class – an aspect of the 5x5x5 research process. Schools and pre-school settings are anxious that they offer equal opportunities and that every child should have the same experience. In 5x5x5 we have seen that by working with a focus research group documentation is realistic and the experience offers learning that can then be applied to the whole class.

In summary, mentors respond to the specific and changing needs of the triangle members, the artist, the educators, and colleagues in the cultural centres. They are ambassadors for the principles of the project and will have a wider understanding of the possibilities of working in this way than new colleagues joining the project. Everyone is unique and builds their own relationship with their colleagues. So far we have not produced a job description although we have held several professional development sessions that have explored the kaleidoscopic role.

How do colleagues think about their mentor?

When colleagues in 5x5x5 were asked about the role of the mentor, all referred to their expertise: '... the intuitive depth of the mentor's understanding of young children', 'her expertise in the early years', 'Her intervention was key. She had a very good understanding of how to put it [5x5x5 project] into practice. She has tools in her tool box which she uses in a very subtle way.'

Support was important for everyone: '... her light holding and gentle presence of being around. This gave a sense of security in which we could explore things.' It was an affirmation and a sense of being valued. Modelling questions was highlighted as a vital technique: '[the mentor's] careful use of questions. She seemed to ask questions at key points making us think what questions we could use. She was modelling questions.' Different and additional perspectives from mentors were appreciated alongside the offer of reassurance. 'The mentor helps to keep us focused when perhaps we are straying.'

Reflective practice

The characteristics of the mentor have much in common with those of the artists (see chapter 6). In her 'poetic essay' researcher Snowber (2005) explores mentoring as an act of deep listening in the way an artist must also listen in the creative process.

> ... [listening] to the specific words, colours, textures and movements which express content, form or lived experience. ... Listening and mentoring are partners in a dance. ...The mentor also works with the human life filled with all its complexities, paradoxes and wonder to "midwife" a deeper enquiry into teaching, writing and living.

At the heart of the mentor's practice is reflective practice. As Schön (1987) describes it, reflective practice involves improvisation, getting in touch with what the child – or in this case the adult being mentored – is actually doing, and the ability to invent methods rather than blindly adhering to just one. His metaphor of jazz is a good example of reflection *in* action. This capacity to take action and use skills 'without intermediate reasoning', being spontaneous, is complemented by the intellectual process of reflection after the event.

Challenges and lessons learned

From ongoing evaluation discussions with all 5x5x5 mentors, the most important challenges and tensions highlight the intricacies of the mentor role. They are listed below.

Are we supporting all corners of the triangle? In most cases the mentors' contacts with the cultural centres have been very limited. The reasons for this seem to be lack of time and some uncertainties about the still evolving role of the cultural centre. Clearly it is challenging to meet the wholly different professional requirements of the three groups involved – artists, educators and cultural centre colleagues. An enquiry into the cultural centres expectations of mentors will be part of research into the role of cultural centres in general. All mentors draw on their own experience but there is a great variety, university lecturers, artists, experienced educators, local authority advisers and colleagues from national charities. They bring different levels of skills and different qualities. How mentors are perceived by the mentees is also affected by their other professional roles. Research in this area and professional development sessions with opportunities for in depth conversations with the mentor team are the most important strategies for deepening understanding.

How do new mentors hook into the culture of 5x5x5 mentoring? The danger of exclusivity among the established core of mentors was recognised, especially in relation to the use of language. As the project extends and new mentors join the team very careful thought will be required in the setting up of appropriate professional development. Each year there will probably be new colleagues joining 5x5x5 from the local authority advisory and consultant teams. They may need support in reframing their professional role towards the more reflective ethos of 5x5x5.

How can mentors be neutral in a project concerned with changing values and practice? Open-mindedness is difficult and mentors need to avoid making assumptions. Given the array of complexities that could be affecting a situation in a school or between the people, they may need to be wary. In their conversations with mentees, mentors need to guard against causing defensive behaviour. Especially in review sessions where colleagues from five local authorities are in discussion there will the danger of confidentiality being breached. Sharing information is part of the review process but everyone needs to be alerted to this.

What is the impact of mentoring? What would count as making a difference, given that we are attempting to change an educational culture? This is part of an on-going quest for the project as a whole. The financial constraints of the project and the demands of other professional responsibilities place limitations on the amount of time which any mentor can give. Very occasionally some mentors have needed more time where difficulties have emerged. We have found that back-up from another mentor can help to share the load.

Mentoring is key in the changing educational culture we are part of. Every mentor needs support and reassurance that change is complex and takes time.

The work of mentoring continues in a changing context

Essentially the nature of the role is one of enabling the participants to reach their potential in their particular setting. The success of 5x5x5 lies in the strength of the collaborative process within a creative learning community.

The collaborative, collegial nature of the project is the key to its success. One mentor commented about the 'building of trust, negotiation, partnership, constructive yet robust interaction' that enables the team to gain deeper insights into learning – to see more possibilities, to be more open to being co-learners with each other and the children. The mentor meetings provided a forum for a support network, and this group too can be reflective listeners with appropriate professional interest, as part of the creative reflective cycle. The mentor's role in research and relationships is subtle. As a team our skills are becoming stronger: as critical friends we are counselling, mediating and we are making our strategies more visible.

The place of uncertainty

Loris Malaguzzi advises that we 'maintain a readiness to change your point of view, so as to never have too many certainties' (Edwards *et al*, 1998). This co-construction of knowledge in a learning community involves valuing each other in a culture of uncertainty, openness and trust. Rinaldi (2006) talks about meaning-making involving 'round table' reflection that can lead to 'crisis' in our own knowledge. In drawing together the threads of thinking through dialogue 'not as an exchange but as a process of transformation where you lose absolutely the possibility of controlling the final result'.

> ... a quality that you can offer, not as a limitation ... to recognise doubt and uncertainty, to recognise your limits as a resource, as a place of encounter, as a quality. Which means that you accept that you are unfinished, in a state of permanent change, and your identity is in the dialogue (Rinaldi, 2006).

In a recent professional development session for mentors, Liz Elders discussed the framework of mentoring in 5x5x5 as a positive place of encounter, of dialogue, of research where our role is to support the exploration of crisis and uncertainty, through our skills in orientation, meaning-making and values.

Liz used Malaguzzi's metaphor of Ariadne's thread to describe the role of the 5x5x5 mentor.

Those who hold the thread, who construct and constitute the interweavings and connections, the web of relationships, to transform them into significant experiences of interaction and communication. (Rinaldi, 2006)

As a group we agreed that uncertainty is an opportunity to make our values transparent, as a reaffirmation of tolerance, confidence, dialogue, trust and relationships. In making explicit reference to the concepts of creative values, transformation and co-construction, together we constructed a frame around the folllowing:

- pillars of rigour, attentiveness and questioning

- ability to hold contradictory states at once – knowing and unknowing

- osmosis – movement between the two states – of knowing and unknowing

- cultural context of support

- researchful minds

If we are to uphold the principles and values of 5x5x5 we need to be open to the concepts of transformation or hybridisation as a result of dialogue. Each year there is transformation – a different story about constant underpinning of values. Each year we revisit these in order to make them explicit and search even deeper.

Digging down deeply into meaning, is a way to learn further, even for people who know a great deal ... the shared construction of meaning, I believe, is the unifying theme of our work. (Filippini in Edwards *et al*, 1998)

e) Evaluation and research
Susi Bancroft and Mary Fawcett

Creativity is notoriously challenging to evaluate. We can generally recognise it, we can talk about it, but evaluating, measuring or assessing creativity is fraught with difficulty. Among the reasons for this is the very nature of creativity which is discussed in chapter 1, and the taken-for-granted ways of thinking about evaluation, measurement and assessment in our society.

We explain how we decided to evaluate the research, then set out the model we use now. We go on to discuss the issues that have been raised and finally suggest ways of moving forward.

What is the 5x5x5 model of evaluation founded upon?

When 5x5x5=creativity was launched our goals were:

- to demonstrate ways in which creativity and innovation can be fostered in and with young children

- to influence early years educational practice by establishing creativity as an essential foundation of early learning

- to share findings as widely as possible, creating a legacy for the future.

In effect we were trying to build a new educational culture, one in which creativity was valued and understood as central to young children's learning and development.

Having a clear set of goals we then had to decide how to evaluate our research. We considered various methods and strategies of evaluation and decided to use the following processes:

- observation
- lightly structured interviews
- documentation of all meetings
- self-reflection through journals
- case studies (see chapter 4)

Providing a structure or framework to encourage researchful attitudes, shared reflective practice and openness to possibilities, required clearcut ethical decisions. We also wanted to develop methods that were practical, useful and manageable for all the participants, and in addition to gather evidence to be used for critical reflection.

One of our principles was to ensure that the process was as democratic as possible, involving everyone as members of our research community. We did not want outside academics to collect evidence for scrutiny. Nor did we want to close down the research through predetermined notions of outcomes to be measured. We saw our methods as a form of action research by the teachers and the artists themselves working in partnership. Indeed we wanted the children too to be engaged in the reflective process. The outcome we sought was much more open-ended and phenomenological than in some action research. What we wanted to know was what actually took place and what people did as researchers into learning when given freedom and permission to be creative, innovative and thoughtful.

There were no precisely defined outcomes- other than the enhancement of everyone's creativity – and we were interested in all the processes. 5x5x5 evaluation was to be 'qualitative, illuminative and formative'.

> **Qualitative**: we focused on establishing what we value as creative action, not on counting measurable elements, and also on processes of research.

> **Illuminative**: we tried to shine a light on to the potentially rich encounters of artists, educators, cultural centres and children and their families so that we could identify and strengthen the capacity of all for creativity.

> **Formative**: we continually drew on our evaluation and reflection to inform further action in our creative and reflective cycle. There is no final end point to researchful practice. However, we did pause at the end of each academic year to gather our findings and assess our progress.

Guiding these essential perspectives about evaluation in 5x5x5 were our principles. Foremost among these was the view of children as creative and competent from birth. A second principle was that we were collecting evidence about a definition of *life-wide* creative capacities, not solely those associated with the arts. Thirdly, we saw ourselves, indeed everyone, as a researcher. Peter Moss calls this 'research as a habit of mind' (Moss, 2003). We were building a research community.

At the start, influenced by the Creative Foundation project of Sightlines Initiative, we defined ourselves as 'researching children researching the world'. After a few years we realised that through our own emerging definitions of what research means in 5x5x5 we were in fact researching ourselves researching children researching the world.

When gathering evidence we are looking for the following elements:

- creative values
- creative relationships
- creative environments
- creative behaviours and dispositions

5x5x5 research continues to be a living process and the structure of these four creative elements emerged over time. They came from reflective analysis and debate about the evidence gathered through documentation.

In our evaluation strategy paper we set out the aspects for evaluation:

- creative environments (emotional climate, time, space, resources) which support the creative activity and thinking of adults and children

- the impact of adults' interventions – artists, educators and cultural centres on the children

- the nature and consequences of the involvement of parents in sharing the process of learning

- the impact of 5x5x5 on the whole school or nursery reflected through the perspectives of colleagues in management and observed changes

- the artists' creative development within 5x5x5 and in their own creative practice

- the development of reflective practice and researchful attitudes among all participants

- the emerging role of arts organisations and cultural centres in supporting the creativity of children and of adults.

Methodology: How 5x5x5 charts progress and collects evidence
The children
Evidence was collected of children's creative behaviours and learning dispositions through observation and documentation of learning stories using many strategies (see chapter 4). Among the learning dispositions noted in the early days were curiosity, willingness to become involved, concentration, collaboration and communication. There was no set list and colleagues continue to identify further dispositions. Some also link their observations to the *EYFS* profile and/or Laevers' Signals of Involvement (Laevers, 2000b).

We collected case studies of individual children which sometimes included evidence of schemas as well as the documentation of creative progress.

Each triangle maintained records or notes of their regular reflection sessions after weekly work with the artist. The importance of shared discussion was emphasised.

The environment

The mentors noted the use of space, resource provision and the use of time before the artist began and on conclusion of their work in that year. Rich discussions about these elements emerged from 5x5x5 practice and lasting changes have been made.

The adults

The mentors discussed key issues about practice with each adult in a semi-structured interview each year before their 5x5x5 work. The light structure enabled the necessary consistency and comparability but also allowed for interesting possibilities for creative debate.

Each adult was encouraged to maintain a personal journal through the year. In it they reflect on changes in their practice, children's thinking and action, their reading and deepening understanding, etc. Artists' journals may also reflect the impact of 5x5x5 on their on personal creative processes and work.

Collaborative relationships

The heart of 5x5x5 practice lies in effective collaborative partnerships (see chapter 3). Differing professional perspectives give rise to exciting possibilities.

Towards the end of the intervention the evaluation team, supported by the mentor, explored:

■   the impact of collaborations between artists and educators in their creative relationships and values through interviews and colleagues' journals

■   collaborations with cultural centres, using a questionnaire

■   the artists network development group (AND) will evaluate the impact on artists practice from collaboration within triangles and within the 5x5x5 community.

How does 5x5x5 share and disseminate the research?

5x5x5 aims to create sustainable embedded practice, to engage with and influence research debates locally, nationally and internationally. We use a mix of methods and opportunities including documentation, exhibitions, seminars, reports, a DVD (*100 voices*) and a website.

- There are layers of sharing the research. Triangle reviews located in the setting, mentor meetings, local authority review meetings, professional development sessions and RED days (Reflection, Exchange and Dialogue) and artists' (AND) professional development meetings are recorded. We search for different ways to make this recording alive, relevant and multiple representational.

- Through presentations, seminars and exhibitions, we make material from records and documentation public. Increasingly colleagues are asked to present our research at conferences across the country. We take part in as many opportunities as possible to contribute to discussions and debates about creativity and learning.

- The annual report draws on all the above sources of data and presents an analysis and summaries of issues. Over the years the report has become a substantial document (Fawcett and Hay, 2003; Bancroft, Fawcett and Hay, 2004, 2005 and 2007).

Issues in evaluating 5x5x5=creativity

Who is the evaluation for?

5x5x5 has been recognised by funders and independent researchers as well as participants for the established strength of its evaluation processes.

The strength and depth of its processes are contained within the core beliefs in the value of the creative reflective cycle, the framework of essential elements and in the documentation making learning visible. Evaluators and mentors are crucial to making evaluation a living process.

In our view evaluation serves the following purposes:

- each adult's personal reflective development on all involved aspects of their 5x5x5 work

- progress within the triangle – collaborative learning

- progress in the local authority group – sharing research

- evaluation information for the whole 5x5x5=creativity community and the Board

■ evaluation information for outside bodies, funders, government, national and international researchers.

If evaluation is to be formative and productive it has to be integrated throughout the research work and seen to be a supportive experience for all participants.

Understanding the meaning of creative experiences
The elements of creativity are broad. With 'possibility thinking' we can identify play, imagination, innovation, risk-taking, posing questions, self-determination (Burnard *et al*, 2006). When observing the elements of young children's creativity with their rapid switching between fact and fantasy and their quick changes in moods and modes, much depends on the eye of the beholder. Subjectivity must always be recognised and care taken in interpretation.

Documentation
Documentation is at the heart of 5x5x5 evaluation. It has led to the compilation of 'treasure chests' of information held both individually and collectively. It is a rich and textured store of data which can be accessed for enquiry into many themes. Fresh discoveries and connections are made possible.

Methodology and models for research
The methodology for evaluation of 5x5x5 is compatible with our vision and principles.

This ensures agreement among colleagues and adds stability and depth to the research. We have however had to explain the value and potential of our 'qualitative and illuminative' methodology. The evaluation structure and processes in 5x5x5 can be considered with reference to both action research and phenomenology. However our approach has certain differences and unique qualities.

Phenomenology
Phenomenology as a research approach aims to show what actually happens in learning situations. It does not set out with a preset question. Observation, discussion and interviews are used to gather material and perceptions of the individuals. A phenomenological approach is not structured by theories and it is inevitably a subjective process. Open-minded unprejudiced attitudes are valued. Hopefully these attitudes allow for clear attentive listening and observation. The art practice of some artists in 5x5x5 relate closely to phenomenological approaches.

The triangles in 5x5x5 attempt to explore assumptions and preconceptions openly. This can result in challenging, dynamic and productive relationships, through which 5x5x5 colleagues can develop collaborative learning. New meanings and knowledge are likely to emerge. However, in phenomenology findings are not interpreted in this way. In 5x5x5 hypotheses, theories, patterns are actively explored and so our style of research differs substantially from that of phenomenology.

Action research

5x5x5 may be thought of as a form of action research. Typically, though, action research begins with a defined question. As we have shown, 5x5x5 encourages research questions which arise from observations of children and through discussions. Our cycles of working involve constant creative reflective review. McNiff and Whitehead (2002) encourage the concept of 'living educational theories'. They emphasise the importance and 'transformative' quality of reflection on individual practice in collaboration with others. Similarly in 5x5x5 each person is encouraged to offer their own descriptions and explanations of learning.

The language and meaning of 5x5x5 evaluation

Inevitably any community starts developing its own language, but in communicating experiences and observation to others we have to be very conscious of the words we use and their often unquestioned meanings. In our discussions with the new Board of Directors there have been debates about what our reports offer: is it 'evidence or data'? what counts as evidence?

Local authorities have other perspectives. They are looking for evidence which connects to their prescribed targets. These too have a language and meaning in context. A current issue is how 5x5x5 engages in these debates. We are investigating how to analyse our data and the impact of 5x5x5 on children's learning and development.

The educational culture of UK

In recent years targets, tests, league tables have all led to a culture focused on summative assessment and quantitative values. In contrast the qualitative research of 5x5x5 has a different ethos and set of priorities. The new *Early Years Foundation Stage* does to some extent bridge the gap with its principles relating more closely to our four evaluation areas. 5x5x5 as an established research initiative has a role in changing the educational culture and fostering the confidence of educators as researchers. Through research, educators learn to interpret and extend initiatives to support children's learning and development.

5x5x5 seeks to link its creative encounters and themes to current relevant research (see chapter 2).

Practicalities

The current grouping of researchers is larger than ever – and expanding. Working with all these colleagues, with 25 triangles there will be over 75 individuals supported by the team of mentors. Meaningful discussions and transformative dialogues take time to develop and nurture so 5x5x5 is considering how best to support the individuals within the group. For evaluation purposes we need to consider the time we require for interviews, reviews, preparing the exhibition and evaluating each year's research within the triangle and wider research community.

The future

We expect 5x5x5 evaluation to continue to focus on the four areas that have developed from research so far. The methodology will be scrutinised over the year and changes may evolve. We expect to develop strength and confidence in being adventurous in both focus and methodology.

Carlina Rinaldi (in Giudici *et al*, 2001) echoes and reinforces the spirit of 5x5x5 in her call for more 'contemporary and alive' research which enjoys emotional and cognitive tension – aspects which produce extraordinary possibilities. Narrating learning makes it exist and pushes our understandings further towards making meaning of experience. It is not always a comfortable place to be. Penny (Director of 5x5x5) often reassures participants that 'it is alright not to know', to trust in the process. Artists in 5x5x5 support this position. Most welcome uncertainty, a heightened state of awareness where tension makes an experience ripe for creative possibilities.

Evaluation for the future will need to match the reframed objects of the charity, which are to advance education by:

- working in partnership with educators and artists, and with museums, galleries, theatres and other artistic and cultural settings to support children in their exploration, communication and expression of creative ideas

- producing and disseminating research and guidance on creative values, relationships, environments and dispositions in order to help children develop as confident, creative thinkers; providing integrated training and mentoring for educators, artists and those involved in cultural settings.

Our principles and practice make research a continually moving process.

f) Professional development
Susi Bancroft and Mary Fawcett

> Professional development: the research and reflection helps me to be more aware of the value of my work and to fine tune it. Normally I don't have time for reflection. Looking at education and finding the language and context to place my practice. Being part of 5x5x5 is proving the worth of what you are doing. Sharing the learning with other settings I am able to be more specific about values. I am able to apply my 5x5x5 work to other contexts. (James, artist, looking forward to the coming year's professional development)

The 5x5x5 concept of professional development encompasses everyone together. All the rich variety of professional experiences among colleagues contributes to deeper understandings and critical thinking about creativity.

This section introduces our principles about professional development and then outlines how we work over the year.

The principles that underpin the 5x5x5 approach
One of our earliest decisions was to bring together educators, artists and cultural centre colleagues for all professional development sessions, both formal and informal. This was because we wanted to try to establish a non-hierarchical, democratic and open community of thinking professionals. We believed that one of the strengths of the 5x5x5 approach was that sharing the different perspectives on creativity, learning and development would be stimulating and productive for everyone. This has undoubtedly proved to be the case. Artists and cultural centres in particular offer insights and different perspectives to what is essentially a learning context. AND has evolved to complement and balance the content of the professional development on offer. This development extends the critical thinking and practice that is open for discussion.

Given the extensive range of professional training and experiences, colleagues will inevitably contribute different forms of expression and varied languages, for example visual, musical, kinaesthetic, psychological, and pedagogical. We hope to explore, develop and extend these differing modes of communication.

5x5x5=creativity is in the process of developing a common language for describing our practice and for discussing it together. If the professional development had been compartmentalised between the different professional groups different languages would probably have evolved. We have become very aware that long-established colleagues of, say, six years use words with

61

increasing sophistication that newcomers are not necessarily familiar with. There can be a real danger of individuals feeling excluded by the language of some debates.

Reflective practice, where colleagues are thinking *in* action and *on* action (Schön, 1987) also enhances meta-cognition, in other words thinking about the very act of thinking. Dialogues with empathetic and informed colleagues stimulate and support the critical thinking, research-focused practice which is our goal.

The principle of collaborative relationships can only be sustained by regular, rich and growing encounters between the triangle members. For this the annual cycle of professional development creates fertile ground.

We avoid the word *training* since to us it carries the notion of instruction and more narrowly defined practice. Our aim is to create a community of re-searchers and learners with self-driven curiosity and enquiry propelling their encounters with the children and each other.

The principles and examples of practice are made clear in our award-winning DVD, *100 Voices* (2006). It has proved a useful tool for professional develop-ment at all levels.

An overview of a year's professional development

5x5x5 professional development takes place in a number of contexts. Some occasions are regular and small scale, whereas some are more formal and less frequent. The levels and formats are discussed below in sections.

The triangle level

In each triangle there are preparatory meetings between the educators and artists before the artist actually begins work with the children. Mentors too, try to attend. These meetings help to establish collaborative relationships and provide opportunities for observing and sharing thoughts about the children.

At this stage the members of the triangle set their 'line of enquiry' or research question for the coming year. Lines of enquiry are helpful in giving a focus, a direction, but they are not rigid. Some examples will help to show the nature of this part of research and professional development. At Batheaston Primary School the research question was 'Where do ideas come from?' At Twerton Infant School they explored 'What does belonging mean?' Bishop Henderson Nursery School, asked 'How are children using movement, gesture, facial ex-pression and words to express themselves and communicate with others?' Moorlands Infant School chose to consider 'What is a creative environment?'

These questions are open and broad. In the 5x5x5 approach we start from children's ideas as far as possible so conceptual questions such as these can be pursued.

Regular weekly review meetings are held after the session with the artist (see creative and reflective cycle). Everyone contributes their observations, reflections, images and interpretations. This leads to a combined group view of the children's explorations, hypotheses, representations and learning dispositions. Notes are made and possible projections for future sessions are discussed. For some colleagues this regular thinking space is quite a revolutionary experience. It is rare to have time set aside in this way. From our experience and from colleagues' comments we know that this is a centrally important mental space for sharing perspectives and understanding the creative learning and potential of the children.

Mentors attend some of these sessions. They will carry out a semi-structured evaluation interview before work starts and again at the end. Colleagues have pointed out how useful they find this as a way of marking their own changing thinking and development.

A whole school approach is important. This has led to professional development sessions for all members of staff located in the particular setting or school. These may be lead by the staff, artist and mentors themselves or by the Director of Research. Similarly, a new group of parents needs to be introduced to 5x5x5 every year. Short meetings at carefully chosen times have proved effective in sharing knowledge about children's creative development, spreading the principles of the approach and bringing in new parent documenters.

The local authority level
Also contributing to professional development are the monthly review meetings of the whole group of settings within a local authority. Currently about five settings take part in each one. Through sharing their triangle's progress with others the educators and artists are developing analytical and presentational skills. The added benefit of comparing their own research findings with their peers' adds to the vitality and depth of the learning experience.

In the first few years we were surprised to discover how much people had in common from their 5x5x5 experiences. This was reassuring and also meant that there could be genuine problem-solving across settings in the local authority whilst allowing time for participants to share their exciting personal researches of children.

5x5x5 has created and taken opportunities to share the research with colleagues across the larger local authority network. In Wiltshire a specific 5x5x5 Forum has been created which involves any interested early years settings and is proving very popular. In other authorities colleagues have spoken at Headteacher meetings and early years conferences.

The whole learning community level
Each year has had a similar pattern of integrated professional development.

Once the triangles have been identified, the equivalent of two whole days in the autumn term, are devoted to initial preparatory development. In the first few years of 5x5x5, when the whole approach was new, we found it was important for senior management and assistants to attend the sessions so that the principles were understood and shared by everyone. Though this is still the case with new settings there tends to be delegation of staff to attend formal sessions.

Planning these sessions is challenging for two reasons. First, the number of people involved has increased dramatically over the years. Now there are typically 25 triangles in action in any one year. In practice this means that 75 or more colleagues may attend. Second, every year some new settings join in and often there are big staff changes. So far there have been virtually no alterations to the team of artists but there have been quite a few additions among the cultural centres. The challenge therefore is to ensure that everyone feels included and fully engaged in the large group. The level of discussion must also be personally appropriate.

We work towards these goals by layering the discussion groups, so enabling everyone to feel that they are contributing and also deepening their learning. We have found the need to revisit key issues every year but aim to develop the ideas at more complex levels. Sessions are planned according to needs identified by colleagues.

New members of 5x5x5 have sessions devoted to their initial needs focusing on the origin and nature of the principles. The activities include opportunities for establishing collaborative relationships and discussing values about creativity.

Each autumn term two days are devoted to professional development sessions with each cohort thus providing opportunities for a dialogue in triangles and local authority groups. We cover a rich variety of content in order to search for shared meanings, challenging the group to consider deep philosophical and pedagogical issues.

RED days: Reflection, Exchange and Dialogue
Two full days or half days are set aside to concentrate on developing themes, fresh research or important background thinking. These sessions have been varied in content in response to needs. This year's RED day was led by the Artists Network Development group and focused on the research perspectives of the artists. We explored links between 5x5x5 and the artists' own professional reflection, practice and development. We noticed the creative interactions between participants and their intense involvement.

Other professional development

The ReFocus network in UK

ReFocus is the UK Network of early childhood educators, artists and others influenced in their practice by the preschools of Reggio Emilia. Its origins lie in the foundation of Sightlines Initiative in 1995 by Robin Duckett.

Initially the focus of Sightlines Initiative was the development of collaborative creative projects at a local level in north east England, taking inspiration from the preschools and infant toddler centres in Reggio Emilia in Northern Italy. Later Sightlines began to organise study trips to Reggio Emilia and became the UK reference point for Reggio Children. It continues with these tasks but also organises regional and national conferences, training, consultancies, advice and support across the UK.

ReFocus, a charity, has been run by a Board since 2004. With funding from Esmée Fairbairn Foundation, the post of ReFocus Development Officer was created to link with regional learning groups, offering advice and support, to members and potential members.

Members of ReFocus are united in their shared perspectives. These are:

- the image of the child as an innate and creative knowledge builder, explorer and co-constructor
- the power of the 'hundred languages' in forming learning environments
- a flexible and creative cycle underpinning the work
- educators and artists as enablers within a pedagogy of listening
- the process of children's exploration as the focus not the end product
- documentation as an important tool in aiding refection and analysis
- professional development as an important part of the whole process

- ■ development of a creative learning community to maintain a continuous supportive dialogue

- ■ family and community involvement not only in the education of children but also for themselves as lifelong learners.

Activities of ReFocus

ReFocus organises international, national and regional professional development opportunities for those working in the field of early years education. It has a membership system and website facility which gives members access to up to date information.

ReFocus has supported the development of ReFocus regions within the UK. There are now eight regional learning groups and seven more are emerging. Each of these support local interest and initiatives and influence policy development. They also enable like-minded colleagues to maintain contact with each other through developing a shared understanding of approaches to early years education.

The Bath and Bristol Group was created primarily by the participants of 5x5x5 =creativity, but it involves other creative learning and teaching initiatives in the area. Our ReFocus group meets three times a year and about 75 people from at least 25 research settings come together with other colleagues in the region. The learning group includes teachers, early years' educators, lecturers, advisers, artists and members of cultural centres. Sessions have focused on visits to Reggio Emilia, the role of the artist, Room 13 (see Souness and Fairley, 2005), documentation and the outdoors. Other professional experiences and development in previous years have included skills workshops offered by the artists and cultural centres.

Our aspirations are to develop a community that is deeply engaged in creative learning: a community of researchers, committed to reflection, exchange and dialogue which includes creative values, integrated creative working practices, professionalism of educators and artist-enablers, co-constructed learning experiences with the children and illuminating and rigorous documentation.

Higher degree level

For two years now qualified teachers have had the opportunity to work towards a Professional Masters degree at Bath Spa University. A special Masters module has been established by the Continuing Professional Development Department and during 2006-7 designated professional development sessions were provided for the educators and mentors. Investigations are in progress to give a similar opportunity for accreditation to artists.

Professional development for artists and mentors
A successful application to Arts Council England South West has given us the chance to research the role of professional development for artists – both in connection with 5x5x5 and their own creative practice. This is being co-ordinated by the AND group (see chapter 6). There is much interest in this research as it is full of exciting and rich opportunities.

The consequences of professional development
This section has tried to demonstrate the ways in which professional development is embedded in all aspects of 5x5x5. It is integrated into practice and responsive to needs identified by colleagues. Some comments by colleagues demonstrate the impact of the 5x5x5 approach to professional development:

> It was so interesting to see the work of other artists, to understand their processes and to see how this relates to the work with 5x5x5. It also felt important to bring a balance between educators' and artists' perspectives so that we can understand each other's languages better. (Annabelle, artist)

Educator Gail from Little Waves Children's Centre, North Somerset said:

> I am much more aware of the importance of time, space and beauty within the learning environment. I am also acutely aware of how my practice in the past has often been overbearing and invasive for children. I am now much more likely to be a quiet but attentive and responsive learning partner working alongside a child than a teacher preaching and probing. I am now content to allow learning to spill out at its own pace rather than using my 'power' to squeeze it out.

> We want the 5x5x5 pedagogy to underpin the practice of the centre. (Redcliffe Early Years Centre)

We have been heartened to see the confidence and success of colleagues that is evident in their higher degree work and we are seeing 5x5x5 leading to career development for a growing number of people. Amongst the educators we have noted how they have moved to positions of responsibility within their own school or local authority and become very effective advocates of the competence of children and how creative and critical thinking are essentially part of sound educational practice.

4

5x5x5=creativity in practice

CASE STUDIES

a) Kinder Garden Nursery
Liz Elders, Deborah Aguirre Jones and Mary Fawcett

The Kinder Garden, a small privately run Nursery in central Bath, offered full day care and education for children aged 2 to 4. It was part of 5x5x5 from the very beginning.

Deborah Jones was their artist throughout. Her professional work as an artist covers performance and a wide range of media, mostly in the outdoor environment. Her processes often include performance and conceptual art – setting up encounters or conversations with other people who may be unconnected individuals or part of a group or an organisation.

Two other artists have collaborated. In year two a film-maker and photographer, Andy Kemp, shared the role of artist and in year three, a sound musician using new technology from WOMAD added another dimension.

The main cultural centre for the first two years was the Institute for Contemporary Interdisciplinary Arts, University of Bath, while WOMAD contributed in year three. As new lines of enquiry grew the local parks were used as a cultural centre too.

Everything was new at the beginning. 5x5x5 itself was starting on its own journey of discovery. What perspectives did the staff of the Kinder Garden have? What was the artist's view of children of this age? How would they actually start the work with the children?

Year One
Early perceptions of young children as learners

This age group was a relatively new one for the artist, Deborah. She saw young children as

> ... wide-eyed, doers and explorers, sensitive and very responsive. My pleasure was in the directness of young children; the children are like material that conducts – like copper with electricity. You see it in the children's faces ... they express it dynamically and vitally.

Liz, the manager and teacher, remembers her changing thoughts about education.

> At college [in the late 1970s] we had been encouraged to think about what education was – 'to lead out' (educare in Latin). But we were warned that in our early teaching careers the government would be setting the curriculum, 'calling the shots'; 'paid by results' was even possible. The National Curriculum arrived and I moved into Nursery teaching. After a few years nursery education itself began to be controlled. Ofsted arrived with the rules, regulations and restrictions – losing sight of the child and what I wanted to be as an educator. I felt constrained and confined.

Liz began to re-evaluate her perceptions of the children and her role as educator. In particular she was examining the processes and role of creativity in young children's development.

> In 5x5x5 these strands seemed to come together and make sense. The project helped me to strip away the accumulated stuff over the years and to go back to my basic principles. I was able to start again with new eye and a decluttered mind. It gave us permission to think afresh rather than stay on the conventional conveyer belt (including Ofsted). I was no longer feeling railroaded.

Making a start

Deborah and Liz tell the story of the first experiences:

With a group of twelve children aged 3 or 4, plus parents and other staff members, we visited the campus of the University of Bath to see Deborah's exhibition and to explore the campus environment, both outdoors and in.

From that excursion we identified key themes that held the children's interest:

- vertical schema
- exploration of space
- an on-going fascination with light and dark

After discussion, which included Anna, one of the teachers, we cleared one room of as much furniture as possible to create an open space free from other activities and distractions. We introduced withy sticks cut from willow saplings as an art-making material. We felt that these had the right physical properties to explore the key themes – they are flexible and can be used to build frameworks and create spaces.

> When they were first presented with a large bundle of withy sticks the children moved back squealing – as if they were excited or frightened. Soon they were holding individual withies and reaching upwards, apparently extending themselves and exploring space around them. (Deborah)

With assistance they went on to bend and join withies. A skeletal structure emerged over two or three weeks, occupying most of the room, and changing shape each week. As we went along mini-explorations were triggered, primarily into:

- taping and joining withies
- cutting
- string and hooks
- tying knots
- moving parts
- holding and lifting things up off the floor

All the while the structure remained unnamed – essentially it served as a hook to hang ideas on – though children often said it was 'like' other things.

> At the end of each day that Deborah worked with us, time was set aside for reflection and planning. These sessions were regularly supported by input from Dan [from the University of Bath, our cultural centre] and our mentor. On these occasions we were able to reflect and respond to tangential projects that took off infectiously across the group. The children often revisited earlier learning and exploration and reused newly gained skills and techniques with growing confidence. Withy sticks developed into flags, birds and kites that the children wanted to fly in the nearby park. An interest in colour was emerging with explorations into colour and light using coloured gels and an overhead projector, and enquiries into drawing itself took place. (Liz)

> I found the sheer complexity of how children enquire striking – there were many layers of thinking and engagement happening simultaneously. For me this indicated the inadequacy of educational approaches which pre-empt activities by separating them into subjects, depicting processes as linear in an attempt to predict and control children's ways of investigating and finding out about the world. (Deborah)

The project in action

The adults seemed to take on different roles quite naturally, though they worked as a team. The artist often suggested materials and contributed technical skills, but the way in which everyone, all the adults and the children, created the action was a fluid and growing process. The artist brought not just materials or skills to this engagement but her thinking, questions, curiosities and sensory responses.

The children turned to any of the adults around. They said: 'We do things and get the grownups to help us with the difficult bits.' The staff always took responsibility for documentation in the early stages.

> This taught us to really look and listen. I can remember being struck by the impressive dialogue of the Reggio children transcribed in their books. It wasn't long before we were also delighted and amazed by the complexity of language and thinking that was coming from our children. There was a constant buzz amongst the staff as overheard conversations and comments were passed on to each other and to the children's parents. Children too were astonished when we reported their words back to them and to the whole group. They were becoming aware that the adults around them valued what they said and did. (Liz)

In the evaluation at the end of the first period of 5x5x5 work Liz noted that the documentation and her observations fed into the *Foundation Stage Stepping Stones* (goals). 'The children are exhibiting skills at a higher level then than they would have in the past, noticeably in: personal and social (collaboration and negotiation); communication, language and literacy; maths; physical and creative development.'

Year Two

Every year each triangle considered their line of enquiry, their research question. At the Kinder Garden in the second year of 5x5x5, with a new group of children, the initial provocation took the form of walks in the nearby Botanic Garden. Armed with cameras and notebooks, adult observations of the children's fascinations identified reflections, surfaces and patterns. Based on these ideas materials were offered – sticks, stones, buttons with which they created patterns and pictorial layouts. Building materials, such as card, tubes, fabric, etc. from the local scrapstore allowed the children to make 3D constructions. Symmetrical arrangements began to emerge.

The photographs of the reflections on the pond, and the patterns made by the sticks and stones on the path intrigued the children. A fascination with maps was spontaneously sparked by Ruby, who drew a map to show how to reach

the Botanic Garden. Andy had joined in by now offering the chance to explore the possibilities of cameras and lenses and how images can be transformed. For example, the mirror feature made remarkable symmetrical images which captivated some of the boys in particular.

Over the next weeks map-making took off, and the floor of a room was papered with an enlarged Ordnance Survey map and the children could drive their toy cars down 'real roads', set up farms, have adventures. However questions were raised. What would be the best scale? Would children connect even more to the map if it was on a bigger scale such as one to one? The children created their own bigger scale map with Deborah. The floor was covered with plain paper to which they added objects and themselves. They were now inside the map.

The mix of play in horizontal and vertical planes through the use of cameras and maps seemed to trigger children's drawing in different ways. They used horizontal and vertical perspectives, aerial views, cross-sectional drawings and more maps. There was an explosion of painting, indoors and out – one child, Molly, even tried to sell her paintings to passers-by in the park! The term concluded with a special exhibition of the children's paintings for the parents.

Every week in the review session the adults reflected on the documentation. From these detailed analyses of the interactions, imaginations, constructed ideas and images, the adults considered how to move forward. The plans were always informed by the children's fascinations and the possibilities for deepening them.

Year Three

There was now a familiarity with the system of reflection and documentation. As Deborah put it 'There was an ease, an 'oh-yes'-ness about it with the children – they seemed to expect the photos, documentation, sharing of ideas.' The adults had been modelling – unconsciously and consciously – a thoughtful style of considering possible ideas and asking questions. A quiet atmosphere of concentration had developed. 'My brain is whispering to me,' said Meggie, before contributing her ideas.

Keeping an open mind about how to make a new beginning with the next year group, the staff were caught by an idea from Tabitha. She was connecting things to make a track for a marble to move along. As she 'walked' the marble along the arc shape she said:

> If I make this longer it will go right across the room and into the next room and it will be like a rainbow. Then it will be like the outside inside. I want to bring the outside inside – the rainbow and the sun. We could have water in the middle and dolphins ...

The staff began to ask themselves questions: 'How can we bring the outside in? How can we create an indoor space outside?' They were sure they needed to research the children's ideas. 'What is the outside? What are its qualities? How does it make you feel? How can we bring it inside?' (see also Austin, 2007)

Over the next few months the children designed a structure with Deborah's support that was freestanding, robust, weatherproof, safe and tall enough to allow adults to stand ('just in case we are allowed in,' as Liz said). At first it was a very temporary one, as they tried out various possibilities. At different times it was a spaceship and a princess's castle.

More challenging was 'bringing the outside in.' The adults debated long and hard how to ask questions to enable 3 and 4 year-olds to think about the abstract notion of the 'outside'. Deep conversations among the whole group began to develop. At one session that the mentor happened to observe, the children were sitting round in a circle debating with each other what the outside was. The depth of their thinking was remarkable. They asked each other questions such as 'How big is the outside?' They remained wholly engaged until they had to stop after 40 minutes. Liz noted that these were children who sometimes could not sit still for a five minute story.

Respect for the children's ideas led to the room being transformed. The children insisted that if they were to bring the outside in they would have to have real grass. And so they turfed the floor.

The room became 'a sensory, theatrical conceptual space, connecting ideas to the wider group of younger children and allowing children to explore through their senses and engage in imaginative role play' (Deborah). This activity was 'bold and inconvenient but the children initiated it all, including stones, logs and plants – all living things and no furniture. They now want the sky!' (Liz). And they found a way to make that happen. The children made a sun which they attached to the light and the adults made a projection onto the ceiling of the night sky and stars.

The classroom environment

Within a few weeks of starting 5x5x5 work it became apparent to the staff that they needed to make changes to both the room and the materials in it. There was no separate room to use and the spaces were fairly small. They aimed to make as much space as possible by removing the superfluous furniture. Previously

> ... the nursery was divided up into areas such as painting and role play and even that was 'parcelled up'. The children had sets of things such as cooking, hairdressers, which were all pre-selected and put into boxes which the children would then set up. ... We wanted to chuck out every bit of plastic. (Liz)

When asked 'What does a creative environment mean to you?' Deborah replied:

> I had in mind a model of an imaginary studio – fairly empty with work spaces, lots of light, almost formless materials which can take on any shape, for example, Plaster of Paris, stone. It will have an openness and spaciousness. A space in which I can be there and leave other things aside, in that space I can make anything.

Now the children know what resources are stored in the nursery, and ask for the things they need to support their play.

Collaborations

In the Kinder Garden the relationship between Deborah, Liz and Anna has been central, a powerful source of creativity and learning for them all. An outer ring of companions and critical friends in their learning made up of Dan (cultural centre), Mary (mentor), Penny (then 5x5x5 research coordinator) and the rest of the 5x5x5 colleagues, have ensured that there were plenty of opportunities for debate and discussion.

The development of creative relationships is subtle and depends on many variables, personalities, understanding, value systems and communication.

Liz describes Deborah as very willing to be open and flexible, not tied to one art medium.

[She]... refers to the wide-eyed-ness of children and her own wide-eyed curiosity. I think that is why Deborah understands them [the children] so well and why the role of the artist is so crucial. The triangle of child – educator – artist as co-investigators becomes so much more powerful. (Liz)

As an artist you are usually expected to pull hats out of bags and to have something which is 'wow!' Projects are usually short-term in which you artificially squeeze what the children do into a 'thing' – learning or product – and it becomes a token. But in 5x5x5 it all belongs to the children – their ownership, their learning about their own thinking. The artist is not distracted by having to do all kinds of other 'stuff' like crowd control, making products and health and safety. This project was most enjoyable, very relaxed.

I feel my role in 5x5x5 discussions, reflections and representing the project has a lot to do with my conceptual sensibilities. This is partly being a participatory artist, where my 'creation' and 'holding' of encounters, events and dialogues is central to my work with performic conversations, building relationships and drawing out dialogue – that's part of my palette of colours, or range of techniques, you could say. (Deborah)

Liz expresses how much she values this contribution from the artist:

It's what is crucial to expanding my way of seeing and understanding. It increases all our sensibilities and leads us to notice and make the interventions in the way that we do.

The artist here has brought a way of thinking, seeing and understanding which is expressed in different words from those used by educators. Between them Liz and Deborah have established a deep connection and a creative partnership.

'Children and adults together have been engaged in a parallel learning journey. We are struck by the similarity of the children's observed interests and those of the artist and educators which has become a passionate partnership of shared enquiry' (Liz and Deborah). Underpinning these partnerships and evident at all levels is a view of the role of adults. Speaking about this after visiting Reggio, Liz described the educator as learner and researcher. She was struck by Carlina Rinaldi's words: 'We can't teach unless we also learn' and also the role of the educator described by a young teacher (in the video *Not just any place*) 'I believe our work is to stand *beside* the children, not *in front* of them, or *behind* them, but at their side and to accompany the children in their discoveries about life and the world.'

Re-educated adults

Liz and Deborah have found the triangle, made up of themselves and the cultural centre, supportive and stimulating. The structure allows for rigour but is not rigid; it is open and permissive and allows for critical reflection. From Dan they learned about cultural theory, the questions, ideas and implications of exhibition curation and the representation of their activities to the children, as part of a reflective cycle, and to the wider public. Between Liz and Deborah there is 'an environment in which you can think aloud, free to bounce ideas around'. Based on their mutual respect and the different perspectives they bring, they explore ideas thoroughly through dialogue and shared practice.

They both acknowledge the transformative experience:

> Its important elements are the stimulation – stretching my abilities, and having a great context to experience and reflect on those abilities; learning about dialogue and collaborative thinking in a context of trust, risk-taking and respect, with thorough and affirmative management structure of the project, co-learning alongside other adult settings. (Deborah)

> We re-invent and re-educate ourselves along with the children. Not only does our knowledge organise theirs, but also the children's ways of being and dealing with reality influence what we know, feel, and do. (Rinaldi in Edwards *et al*, 1998)

Challenges

To the outside observer this setting's collaboration between artists and educators seemed to flow almost effortlessly, but there were aspects which presented challenges.

Documentation

The making and gathering of daily notes became routine, but how to store and re-represent regularly and effectively for the children and other people was an on-going challenge.

Time

Management of time is crucial and sometimes difficult – what to prioritise, how to make best use of the artists' time when they are there. Deborah wished her time with the children was more continuous; she still feels like a visitor only coming in twice a week. The nursery does pursue the children's interests in her absence but greater continuity would be desirable.

Grouping the children

Sometimes the adults have discussed their concern about working with only a few children, but they have observed the way in which fascinations and types of play do spread to the rest of the group, even to the younger children, who are not in the same room.

In many 5x5x5 triangles educators have tried to be inclusive and democratic, but working with a whole class (say 30 children) usually 'dilutes the quality of the experience, how it functions and the capacity of how far the process can reach – on a sensory, conceptual level, and probably educational too' (Liz).

At the start it is clearly best

> ... to allow the project to immerse itself in a small group's explorations which not only allows the relationships to develop (so that the artists know the children as people, not just names and crowds), but also enables us to notice and enter into a whole other level of intelligent enquiry that the children are conducting, As we continue to work with this small group with 'real' relationships and enough attention to space to notice the really surprising actions/intentions/inquiries, then our quality of engagement (in noticing ourselves as much as noticing the children) goes up a few notches. Somehow this is recognised by the children, and it seems as though it can spread throughout the nursery, to other children and adults not directly involved with the project. So being 'undemocratic' does actually turn out to affect the whole setting. (Deborah)

The staff in the Kinder Garden were actually engaged in the reflective cycle throughout the whole week, even when the artist was not there. The ethos of enquiry, child-informed work, observation and reflection never ceased.

Staff development

From the early days of the project Liz ensured that the whole nursery team understood the principles – listening to children, being informed by their interests, concentrating on facilitating open-ended play and the hundred languages of children. With the arrival of several new staff members professional development had a higher profile. For Liz this way of working was embedded in everyday conversation and practice and she herself provided a model of 'mindful' practice. The new members learned through example and the non-threatening, supportive environment.

Being a 5x5x5 artist

Deborah often refers to the 'language' of 5x5x5 being educational, albeit a radical model of education. The project's aims, motivations, reference points and measures are different to those of an artist. Practitioners find plenty of overlapping areas, but there is a danger, she says, 'that I'll disconnect at some internal level and drift away if the work loses relevance to the inquiries of my practice.' Different professionals from different worlds have different perspectives, language and values (see further discussion in the chapter 6 on the role of the artist).

Visiting professionals

One of the sound musicians who participated in the outdoor work epitomised certain problems.

> He didn't have an understanding of the depth of thought of the children. This heightened our appreciation of long-standing relationships. He had not had the benefit of the professional development; he showed no understanding of where the children were coming from. If you don't know the children it is very difficult to respond sensitively and appropriately. (Liz)

In conclusion

> I'm amazed at the sophistication of the children's research – exploring the outdoors through their bodies and senses, representing its qualities through metaphor and having conceptual understanding of it. These things inform my practice as an artist. (Deborah)

> Whilst this (5x5x5) was a very scary thing to take on, because we had to change our perception of our roles and children's capabilities, three years on we feel it's a more natural and pleasurable way of working. Now I've made the mental shift, I don't see myself as a 'teacher' in the conventional sense – we're here to help them explore and discover the world in a way that actually means something to them. (Liz)

Liz describes herself 'as a protagonist, co-researcher and co-learner' with the children and the other adults. Deborah sees her role as thinker and conceptual explorer. Both have confidence and trust in each other. Those of us who have had the privilege to observe their dialogue are beginning to understand their creative, researchful partnership.

The Kinder Garden closed in July 2006 but Liz Elders' and Deborah Jones' involvement in the research of 5x5x5 continues.

b) Twerton Infant School
Anna Ashby, Jayne Rochford Smith and Mary Fawcett

Twerton Infant School is in its fifth year or research with 5x5x5=creativity. This case study indicates the depth and value of a long-term research relationship.

The school is situated in south Bath in an area with predominantly council housing. It has links with two 5x5x5 settings, the local Children's Centre and Lime Grove Special School.

Amy Houghton, a multi media textile artist, has worked with the reception classes. Her research and practice involves exploring how we use and read antique textiles and photographs as stimuli for nostalgic longing and as indicators of our authenticity. She has been exploring the processes of playful discovery and creation of narratives from the reading of evidence of events and happenings evident in the impressions, use and age of objects. Amy has experience with special needs work and as a documenter in 5x5x5.

While Amy was studying for an MA at Goldsmiths College, furthering her research and practice, Tess Richardson Jones, an illustrator of children's books and an experienced artist working in early years settings, took on the artist's role.

The Hotbath Gallery and The Royal Photographic Society have been the 5x5x5 cultural centre partners.

Year One
A challenge
The intention was for the two schools, Lime Grove Special School and Twerton Infant School to work in partnership with alternating visits each way. The Infant School children spent a first stimulating session in the multi-sensory light room at Lime Grove, and thereafter children from Lime Grove visited the reception class at Twerton Infant School.

The organisational logistics were very challenging. Staffing ratios had to be high for making the journeys and supporting the children in each environment. Management of the timetables of both schools was tricky. For some of the children with special needs life in the busy reception class was daunting. Inevitably it took time for everyone to get to know each other.

Since 5x5x5 depends on a creative and reflective cycle of planning and reflection, that too had to be fitted in. Everyone was dedicated and generous with their time.

The artist

For each session Amy provided a rich variety of fabrics, tapes, card, – raw materials which Reggio colleagues call 'intelligent materials'.

> When the children were first presented with the materials they went wild! When they realised [the materials] weren't going away they stopped being in a rush and took their time. (Jayne, teacher)

> They started by really exploring the new equipment and materials with excitement and then they focused on their discovered interests. Once they had adapted, the children took control – they asked for things and used the adults as a resource. (Amy, artist)

To the adults an unexpected result of this growing self-confidence and initiative-taking was the regular incorporation of the home corner – which was not planned for the 5x5x5 work – into the children's play. This was fantasy play using all kinds of elements, both actual and imaginative (see chapter 4).

Collaborative relationships

Relationships in this triangle quickly became supportive. The project became a passion. The school provided exceptional back-up support – a technician helped and the head teacher too regularly supported in the use of computers and the flow of images.

> There was no suspicion, or wariness – there was trust. Our relationship just worked, unspoken. Jayne carried on the project through the week, keeping it alive, sharing feedback. There was not the pressure for the artist to work alone or to wave a magic wand and get the children to produce a presentable piece of art. The focus was much more about the children's learning. (Amy)

Documentation

At Twerton the pattern was for Jayne to show photographs, taken at the morning session with the artist, to the children in the afternoon for them to reflect on and to talk about.

> It proved to be a good way of getting the children's feedback, views and opinions of what they were doing and a chance to ask the children questions that sometimes were untimely to ask when they were involved in their activities. (Amy)

Changes in practice

Over the first year Jayne noted that though her organisation had always been fairly flexible, it was now much more so and she felt confident about giving the children more time. Her practice now involved more observation and response to children's interests and ideas.

The range of basic materials became more extensive and was made easily available to the children.

Professional development
Amy said 'I am interested in exploring creativity ... I want to understand the qualities I have as an artist. It has been an enabling experience.' Her interest in this age group together with the integral nature of young children's learning developed. Amy also regarded doing presentations of her work as an artist as 'fantastic practise' and strengthened her confidence to start work on a higher degree.

Cultural Centre
Stacey Crawshaw from the Hotbath Gallery assisted with documentation on some occasions and with the exhibition at the end of the year – she had professional design and presentation skills. The class also visited an exhibition at the gallery. After looking at the exhibits the staff offered yellow post-its on which the children did drawings and which they then they stuck up on the wall in the gallery, making their own immediate exhibition. Amy said 'the visit was absolutely magical, fantastic. The children surprised me, they sustained interest for a long time.'

Year Two
The new element for the second year was to integrate sessions with a musician, John Walls, supported by Mandy Adams from Womad (World of Music, Art and Dance). This was funded by *Youth Music* and is discussed further in chapter 4.

Relationships
The quality of sensitive collaboration deepened over the second year. Amy said 'Jayne and I work so well together ... a natural equal relationship where there is an expectation to bounce ideas off each other.' In sessions they developed a system, Amy being responsible for photographs and Jayne for taking notes (though there were others documenting too) – they communicated with each other through quick eye movements and pointing. Amy said 'Jayne has flexibility and an amazing skill and openness to new ways. I feel I can say what I feel. I don't have to be polite. I can voice any concerns knowing it won't get a defensive response.' They were both open to different strategies and never had a sense of failure even if things did not proceed as expected. And both acknowledge the strong mentoring support from Pam throughout the year.

Year Three

This was the year that Tess Richardson Jones worked as artist whilst Amy was away studying for her MA. The adults chose as their research question 'What is belonging?' This opened up various areas of enquiry.

The focus began with children's families and the adults organised a parents' coffee morning. Jayne showed videos of role play and photographs of exploring; she also explained about the resources they used and which the parents could see and handle. She and Tess talked to the parents about the 5x5x5 research.

The importance of maintaining links between the families, children and the school were discussed. The aim was building bridges in the community and encouraging parents to contribute to the children's researches and explorations. The level of interest and support for the idea of an 'ongoing noticeboard' and further coffee mornings was very encouraging.

Mir's mum: 'Having things like this makes me feel part of the school.'

Joseph's mum: 'It helps me to know what they are doing.'

Morgan's mum: 'When Morgan asked to take things in from home I said no because I didn't understand. This really helps me to support him.'

Later Jayne commented that they had underestimated the parents of these children and that engaging them more closely was 'an education for us all'.

The adults thought about children and their families belonging to the local community, and took the children to the regular local market. The children demonstrated their sense of belonging in the locality as they walked along identifying who lives in this house, people they knew, photographing each other's faces and their expressions, leaving messages for each other. They also reacted with interest to the weather and the changes it was causing – the sun melting frost, leaves falling from the trees even though there was no wind. They loved being in a group of their peers on an expedition and exploring together, but interest in the market was limited!

Back in the classroom every child was given a shoe box for messages which they personalised. Making messages (often on yellow stickers), delivering or sending them – to the head-teacher, other members of staff, each other – was an absorbing theme. Later when a child left the school they created a special one for their friend. How to get the box across the city to their friend at his new school was the next challenge. Fantastic ideas were eventually superceded by the possibility of really using the Post Office. This was another absorbing expedition through the local streets, preceded by much writing of messages and wrapping up.

In reflecting on the sense of belonging the adults recognised it was influenced by group size, composition, relationships, cooperation, sensitivity and communication. They decided to focus on a small group of children and to keep their provocations open enough for the children to interpret in their own ways. The messages theme continued but some individual children became more engaged by and more capable in their use of photography.

What were the key changes that had taken place by the end of the third year?

Timetable and organisation
Planning is now different.

> Apart from literacy and numeracy we now record what has been done rather than what we are going to do. We realised that we didn't always have time to cover everything shown on previous plans. It is more work now, but much more meaningful. (Jayne)

They have the total support of their head teacher. 'Working with an open timetable takes away the 'rush element', we have different priorities' (Jayne). The adults became very aware of the structure of time. It was essential to allow clear blocks of time for exploration and representation of ideas.

Children's ideas
Supporting children's ideas means that the work is now more individual. Staff are much more aware of different learning styles, for example the highly vocal children and the observers. Typically they mind-map a new theme together with the children.

Space and materials
Staff are now more selective than they were about materials. They tend to see the space as a 'blank canvas' with different resource areas, such as mark-making, construction, role play.

Observation, documentation and reflection
Jayne attributed the transformation of their perceptions in large part to fresh, unprejudiced observations. The artists with whom they worked, in contrast to teachers, 'brought a whole different perspective, not a baggage of prior knowledge like teachers – all target-based.' The staff are all now observing and documenting what the children are really doing. Jayne frequently asks herself 'what is the learning, the purpose of this, the gain for the child?'

The teaching assistants had to learn how to document too and one now advises students. The staff are constantly reviewing their observations and reflections and once a fortnight there is time set aside for a thorough review time. They find themselves questioning each other and everything they themselves do.

> We are willing to change and not feel a failure. Something always comes out but not necessarily what is expected. We have no fear of stepping back and watching. (Jayne)

Professional development
> The issues that the children have been exploring have been quite fundamental to building identity and feeling confident in your own skin. The issues are the same for the children as for the adults. My fascination with philosophical issues is constantly growing. ... The learning journey I am making with the children is a professional development in itself. (Tess, artist)

Concluding thoughts at the end of Year Three
Tess and Jayne found the children had become more independent. There was a change in their responses to each other which as Tess described as 'less confrontational, valuing each other's ideas, wanting to include less vocal children'.

> The children are more patient with each other and are sensitive to the needs of different children. They are less competitive, not fighting to be centre of attention. (Jayne)

> The children never cease to amaze me with their ingenuity, enthusiasm and resilience. I feel that I'm one of the gang working alongside them and my role is supporting and noticing when I can enhance the experience by adding materials, etc. to extend their investigation. (Tess)

Whole school development: December 2007
5x5x5=creativity has been a catalyst for development across the whole school. Long term changes in philosophy and practice led by the head teacher evolved over the last four years.

In her Masters degree essay Jayne identifies key aspects which have transformed her practice – and that of the rest of the school. These include: truly valuing children, the importance of autonomy, creativity at the heart of early education experiences, listening to children, documentation and reflection.

> It is interesting as a school to think back to our perception of creativity before we started the 5x5x5=creativity project. Within school certain individuals, adults and

children, were referred to as being 'creative' meaning showing an interest and 'talent' for the arts. Creative activities within school were often adult led involving producing a set outcome, for example a copy of Van Gogh's Sunflowers, and creative activities were definitely considered as arts based. Other individuals would comment on their lack of creativity, often an opinion which had been embedded in them during their school years.

I would see creativity for everyday life (Craft, 2002) as the backbone within our curriculum development within school. I also feel this sort of creative attitude ignites an excitement and aptitude for learning. One could also say the changes and challenges created by re-developing the way we teach had opened up the 'little c 'creativity in the adults working within our school.' Critical reflection has been heightened, specifically on my own teaching practices and the interpretations and deductions I make about children and their learning.

Anna, a reception teacher who has now been involved for over a year, writes in her MA essay:

- I now work collaboratively with other adults and children and have become a role model of collaboration.

- I now see professional 'risk taking' as a positive and exciting possibility.

- I have discovered a new way of documenting the learning process and moved away from measuring predefined outcomes. 'Assessment for learning' has been promoted as a result.

- I have developed a 'curriculum' with the children based on their own interests and fascinations. Planning has become retrospective and therefore responsive to the children's needs and more creative in its approach.

- Priority is given to 'key skills' such as perseverance and persistence in order for children to become 'lifelong learners'.

- I now view myself as a 'co-constructor' and 'protagonist' of knowledge and am no longer a dictator.

- The environment has become 'inviting' or 'potentiating' and is set up to promote quality interactions between pupils.

- Careful consideration is given to the resources provided, 'intelligent and open ended materials' have been found to be the most effective in stimulating children to learn, ensuring they are 'ready, willing and able'.

Together Jayne and Anna write about the consequences of their school's refocused approach to learning:

- Children developing powerful skills in questioning, problem solving and investigating. They tell us what they want to learn!

- Children in control and excited by their learning

- Children's improved behaviour and increased self-esteem

- Collaboration both with children and adults -working together to solve problems, share resources and ask each other's opinion and advice

- Children believing in creative possibilities – an anything is possible culture

- Parents supporting understanding and interested in what children are doing

- Children's concentration and interest increased

- Children's improved attainment now evident in *Foundation Stage Profile* and *SATS* results that are now above the national average.

What's brilliant about 5x5x5=creativity is that it respects the way children learn and values them as learners in their own right. At Twerton we have witnessed the direct results of this recognition: the children have learned more powerfully across all areas of the curriculum and made huge strides in their self-esteem. (Paul Mattausch Burrows, Headteacher)

c) St Saviour's Nursery and Infant School
Ed Harker and Mary Fawcett

St.Saviour's Nursery and Infant School in Larkhall on the outskirts of Bath has also been with 5x5x5 from the beginning. For three years the artist in the school was a drama specialist, Sasha Laskey, and the cultural centre was the Theatre Royal Bath where Kate Cross was working towards the establishment of the egg children's theatre. The children were in the two reception classes in the Foundation Stage.

Getting started

The teachers thought role play would be an interesting area of creative learning to explore. The idea of starting with a visit to the Theatre Royal was appealing. The staff took all the children in the Foundation Stage, in two groups, to visit the theatre, where they explored every aspect of the building. By analysing the children's reactions to and memories of the trip the staff found that some children were keen to make model theatres and others wanted to present their stories as shows. Children who showed particular enthusiasm or interest in these themes were selected to make up two focus groups, and they worked with Sasha. 'Our earlier adult suppositions about the most 'interesting' areas of the Theatre for the children were wrong, and this is a lesson we still enjoy re-learning on a regular basis' observed one of the teachers.

The Foundation Stage staff began a deeper enquiry into make-believe, role play and the concept of performance. Over several years classroom practice changed throughout the school as a consequence.

Changing the environment
The most significant change to the environment in the first year was the abandonment of specifically themed role-play areas and props such as rockets, castles, fireman outfits, princess's tiaras and the creation of a larger and more flexible space in the heart of the classroom. The new role-play props were very simple, such as pieces of fabric, sticks, and a few large hollow bricks. (For more about the learning story of 'The four beasts and the one Dad with no child' see *ReFocus Journal*, 2005)

Year Two
Choices
Choices had to be made for Sasha's work in the second year – which school spaces to use and how to give the opportunity to as many children in the two

reception classes as wanted to take part. The staff had to decide what criteria to use to select the focus groups. How could they make the selection transparent and justifiable to the children, parents and other adults involved? They also wanted to ensure that the ripples of the 5x5x5 work penetrated the whole school.

As the year progressed their choice of the school's under-used conservation area as a focus for the work raised its own question: how can planned provocations compete with the wonders of nature?

The adults had refined their research into one simple question: 'What is make believe?' After exploring the school conservation area with its pond, bushes and trees, the focus chosen was: who, real or imaginary, might live in the area. Dramatic stories with monsters and other fantasy creatures emerged naturally, but some were also prompted by adult-selected materials.

At first the adults made small provocations such as creating stick dens and leaving 'evidence' of mysterious inhabitants, but the children tended to explore and invent according to their own imaginative fascinations.

Groupings
Experimentation with various groupings – single gender groups, a mix of personalities, quiet children with the more energetic – offered interesting observations and much discussion which often surprised the staff. Their expectations about gender differences were confounded – the boys used sticks as wands, while the girls chose to turn the sticks into weapons and became 'mud monsters'.

Parents
Parent documenters began to support the work. They joined the sessions after they had attended an evening meeting in school which explained 5x5x5 and asked for help with documentation. As one of the teachers said:

> The parent documenters have learned about how children learn and the way our school does things. They see that it is not just playing. It has been a big eye-opener. Even having just a few parents involved has had a strong and positive ripple effect on other parents.

These developments synchronised with the whole school moving to a more creative approach to teaching and learning.

Knowing the children

The teachers discovered new insights into the children they thought they already knew. One noted that 'the 5x5x5 work in the conservation area has been particularly good for children who are constrained in the four walls of the classroom.'

Year Three

The line of enquiry

The line of enquiry 'What is make-believe?' continued to develop. Sasha and the staff decided to refine their research question, and to ask 'What is magic?' 'Magic' often featured in the children's explanations of how role play worked. The team chose to use a defined space within school since the natural world was too great a competing interest.

Grouping the children

The adults' criteria for selecting children for the focus group included the children's enthusiasm for role play, and their ability to connect with other children and to build on the ideas of others.

The story

In the third year Sasha chose an inspiring story as a starting point for the work, 'The Kelpie King and the Sea Horse'. She felt that the story would become 'the backbone or platform – it gave the children the structure to build off.'

The sessions were more structured than in the year before. They began with a warm-up using drama games, then the story work took place, and finally the children reflected on the afternoon's experiences using a wide range of creative media such as drawing, painting and construction.

The visit of the Kelpie King

As time went on the children became particularly interested in the somewhat scary fantasy figure of the Kelpie King. To challenge the stereotype of the baddie Kelpie King and encourage the children to question why a character would behave as he did, a professional actor was hired to become the Kelpie King.

The conversations about where he came from, whether he was real, and whether the Kelpie Queen was a goodie or a baddie, continued through both reception classes, and still provokes interest several years later!

Play: a total experience

The children became deeply involved in the fantasy, role-play and art activities. The adults felt that they had begun to answer their research question – much of the magic of role-play comes from story and narrative.

The question of how adults involve themselves appropriately in the children's realm was debated. Sasha felt that fantasy role play required the adult to be totally involved in the flow and immersed in the children's emerging stories. Self-consciousness would strike a false note and prevent her from sustaining the children's threads of thought. The artist needs to feel at one with the children's thinking and their deep immersion in fantasy. Sasha achieved this, but pointed out that when '... you are very involved yourself, in the flow yourself, immersed in role, you can not also document'. But can you document effectively without being involved?

A parent who was preparing to return to teaching took on documentation throughout the year and her valued observations and contributions were shared in the weekly reflection sessions.

Reflections on the experience

One teacher reflected 'I am now realising how much you don't know about children. As a teacher you only see what they choose to present'. Through allowing the children to explore their own fascinations 'children reveal themselves, they are relaxed enough to share'.

Sasha found 5x5x5 liberating: 'I had permission to really listen to the children and to value their contribution'. She felt that the project had created a safe environment in which children can take risks.

The teacher noted: 'There is a stable foundation, a bedrock, of routines and relationships. Only then can you get revelations'.

Both adults believed that 'adult involvement is a sensitive engagement and a subtle interplay.'

> Sasha: 'In 5x5x5 the creative work comes out of the relationship'.

> Teacher: 'We create the environment that allows and encourages the child to share their ideas, and help them to make connections'.

> Sasha: 'It was important to work over an extended period of time where there isn't a pressure to achieve something in the short term'.

Kate Cross acknowledges that engaging with 5x5x5 added to her understanding about working with young children which has in turn impacted on the development of *the egg* Children's Theatre at the Theatre Royal, which opened in the autumn of 2005.

> Sasha: 'We have always felt we're trusted [by 5x5x5's research team].'

> Teacher: 'We have felt trusted by Denise, the school's head teacher.'

Year Four

The question this year was 'How do stories support learning?' Using the 'Story Square' technique (Paley, 2004) gave the adults a structure which allowed children to be really heard. The model succeeded in drawing out children's individual stories and fascinations, and it also supported their acquisition of a basic grammar of drama. But working with many separate stories made it much harder to create an extended enquiry. The vital collaborative nature of the previous year's projects was missing.

Year Five

The triangle was completely new for Year Five, with new teachers, a new visual artist, a new cultural centre (Swainswick Explorers, an environmental group of the Forest School type) and a new mentor. The whole year group made weekly visits to a stream and hillside within easy walking distance of the school, helping to ensure that the discoveries made by the smaller research group of children could be widely shared. However the winter weather was against them – it was wet and cold. Their research revealed the power of the natural environment just as it had in Year Two, with the children naturally drawn to explore the stream repeatedly. Sensitive observations and subtle interventions reinforced the finding that the children could be satisfied with little more than this.

The longer term result of the year's engagement is that children now go regularly to this wonderful natural resource on their doorstep, and that future 5x5x5 work will be planned to make the most of the finer weather in spring and summer.

Impact on the school

The school has always been an open and engaged place. To attribute all the changes which have taken place to 5x5x5 is perhaps not the whole story. However, the environments, the reflective cycle, documentation and display have all evolved. Now every class – nursery, reception and years one and two – has a role play performance area. 5x5x5 work demonstrated the need for a flexible work space in school and this has been created. Known as the 'small hall' it is open and flexible and is used in many ways. Another aspect of the environment, the use of the outdoors, has developed and become a regular fixture on the timetable.

A reflective learning cycle is regularly used in curriculum planning through the school. The school has been influenced by the work of Belle Wallace, though her 'TASC wheel' method is not used in 5x5x5 sessions.

The use of documentation continues to evolve. The value of good quality documentation is now recognised as a strategy for informing parents, children and other adults. As new technologies such as digital cameras have become cheaper and more accessible, so much more is possible. The school has installed several computer screens facing out through the school windows, so allowing digital displays and documentation to be seen by parents and carers at the start and end of the school day, and by the children during it.

Child-initiated learning is recognised and a specified time for it is built into the timetable. The enquiry led work of 5x5x5 has also heightened interest in *Philosophy for Children* (P4C).

The headteacher talks now of a 'mission to explain' the ways that the school works with the children, and feels strongly that by sharing these principles and practices with the wider community their impact will be more secure.

d) John – a child study
Karen Wallis

This case study is about my interaction as an artist with one child. It demonstrates the beneficial impact that 5x5x5 can have on a child who is having difficulty in relating to his peers. It has been written in collaboration with Jane, the class teacher.

Following our first 5x5x5 research together, Jane and I agreed our second research question: 'What makes a creative environment?' Our theme was collecting and looking at things that were 'special'. This theme was to be explored with all the children in the class but in order to research responses in more depth, six children were chosen to work in a group with me in the corridor outside the classroom, with a parent and the class teacher as documenters.

The children were chosen because they all had some degree of difficulty in relating comfortably to other children in the class. Jane felt they had not yet found a voice to express themselves easily in school and thought that they would particularly benefit from working in a quieter space with careful adult attention and support.

The first provocation was a 1.5m square of paper fixed onto the corridor wall and a supply of good quality pastels. The children were invited to draw things they felt were special. They all seemed happy to engage with the activity and worked well together over the whole paper until the end of the session. Jane observed that John seemed noticeably more at ease than usual in the company of the other children. He scarcely interacted verbally but positioned himself physically much closer to other children than he usually liked to, calmly drawing shoulder to shoulder with the others.

At first I was unaware that John had any difficulty relating to his classmates. He dutifully took part in all activities and did nothing exceptional. I began to notice him more when we visited the museum, which was our cultural centre. Although not enthusiastic about being in the museum, he did an excellent observational drawing of a clock.

His attitude in the next session was quite different. It began with Jane showing the whole class pictures of the museum trip, followed by some of her own china treasures. Afterwards, John made a richly decorated plate, using an innovative choice of materials and was totally absorbed for the whole session. Afterwards, I went into the playground to watch my group. John seemed happy; he was making up games and showing them to the others. Jane commented that this calmer behaviour in the playground marked a significant change for John.

For some time he had been having problems in playtime, which had become an increasingly negative experience for him. He usually became entangled in rough physical games, often of his own choosing initially, but which he found hard to manage. He often ended up hurting or being hurt, and Jane and his mother were meeting regularly to monitor the situation. He may have drawn negative attention onto himself through his own expectation of trouble and he might also have been affected by stereotypical boys' behaviour, thinking that he should play rough games in order to fit in with the other boys. In many cases his anxiety prevented him from knowing when to stop being rough. Clearly a sensitive child, his outdoor aggression did not match his indoor sensitivity.

Jane informed me of the shift in John's behaviour since the first 5x5x5 session. Thus alerted, I observed him closely to see if the 5x5x5 sessions had any further effect. He continued to take part in all the activities, with compliance but no noticeable enthusiasm. However, a week or so later we had a significant conversation. John had opted to draw a treasure map – which didn't take him long. Before he went back into the classroom, he told me that he found everything boring. We talked about this and I asked him to tell me when he thought of something that would not be boring. As he went back into the classroom he looked back round the corner and said: 'Boring, boring, boring!' Although he might have been exaggerating for effect, I decided he needed a challenge.

In consultation with Jane, I opened up the afternoon sessions to the whole class – not just my selected group. The 'open house' was enthusiastically taken up by many children – but John did not come out that day.

The following week I added some 3D elements to the corridor: a curtain of green cellophane and some bubble-wrap over a small wooden frame. John came out willingly. He played with the cellophane and the bubble-wrap and then settled down to draw. I let him take his own photo of his drawing with my camera. He clearly enjoyed this and I gave him a print of his photo to take home. But once again he did not take part in the open session.

Opening up the afternoon sessions to all seemed to sharpen John's sense of possession in the project. Although he continued to stay away from the open sessions, he would check what was going on. More significantly, he made a full commitment to the 5x5x5 sessions in the mornings.

One session, there was a particularly physical role-play activity. I realised that John had lost his comfortable attitude and ability to be creative. From then on

Yes I took that. That's Spider Man. That one I took home.

we channelled his energies towards more thoughtful, perceptive activities. He developed a balance of physical, clowning play alongside drawing or making, which sustained his interest. He also helped develop the decoration of the corridor and began to involve others in his play. The art works he made demonstrated considerable ability and at review time in the classroom John no longer acted cool but was keen to show what he'd made.

During the penultimate 5x5x5 session, John made another significant shift – from creative activity into creative leadership. I had covered the corridor sky-lights with coloured cellophane and laid a strip of newsprint along the floor to catch the colours. John decided the paper had to be drawn on and began to make the paper strip into a train track. He soon realised that he could not manage to draw the whole length of the paper (about 10 metres) so he enlisted my help, giving me clear instructions on what to do: 'Draw six lines,

John: 'I'm looking through there. (Laughs) You'll be in my head that'll be there and you'll be looking at me!'

then change colour' (to echo the colours on the skylights). He then enlisted the help of three other boys. Although they deviated from his instructions, John allowed and agreed to their variations. Together we completed the task by the end of the session.

John was clearly upset by the prospect of 5x5x5 ending, although he hid it behind a brave face. We let the children decide what to do for the last session. John came up with a definite plan so we followed that and let him lead a parade with painted balloons round the school grounds.

From his mother we know John likes doing school work and art work at home but doesn't know when to stop, because he doesn't like the things he loves to come to an end. He has talked enthusiastically about 5x5x5 at home. His mother thinks he appreciates the one to one attention.

Oh yeah – that was drawing the track ... Drawing, drawing, drawing...

From Jane's point of view, 5x5x5 has made a significant impact on John. His playground difficulties stopped completely once he was involved in 5x5x5 and he became able to be with others in shared activity. He gradually grew more talkative as the sessions progressed and started sharing his interests. He developed the confidence to take a lead and then to take a management role. John's image of himself changed from someone who had to comply with 'what boys do' to someone with a role as an instigator and explorer. 5x5x5 gave him the outlet and thus facilitated that shift.

Postscript

After my 5x5x5 sessions ended, Jane told me that John showed minor signs of regression to his former pattern of playground behaviour but that she was easily able to pull him back. We were keen for him not to lose the benefit of 5x5x5 so this year (2008) I have continued with the same children, now in Year 1. John's new teacher tells me he is very bright and has to be kept interested when he finds school work too easy. He is clearly delighted to be doing 5x5x5 again and is ready and eager for every session. His facility to lead is still in evidence and I feel we are now working in a partnership.

LEARNING STORIES

a) Freshford Primary School
Tessa Richardson Jones, Catharine Naylor and Sam Mosley

Artists have worked in partnership with the reception class of 4 and 5 year olds at Freshford Primary School for four years, with new children each year. The artists are Catharine Naylor and Tess Richardson Jones and the class teacher Sam Mosely. The headteacher, Anne Forrest has been actively engaged with 5x5x5. She says '5x5x5 is very special. The people involved really listen to the children, valuing what they say and want they want to do.'

The initial stimulus was provided by the artists taking the children on a walk. The goals were to observe the children's fascinations, to listen to what they had to say and to get to know them better. The idea for a museum came from the children and all the quotations which follow are theirs. Although the artists provide basic materials for drawing, constructing and making, they are perhaps more important as catalysts, creating a climate supporting the children's and adults' creative development.

Here is how the artists describe the museum learning story.

Making a museum 2007
Discarded objects, including a beach ball and a rusty tin, were found among feathers, pine cones, shells and sticks, all fascinating in their incongruity, all picked up and brought to the classroom. This triggered interest in collections and was a source of inspiration for fantasies to take root and grow. Fragments of the walks were sometimes brought back in the form of memories, photographs, and sounds. The classroom became a space to share 'treasures', to talk about their meanings and connections, taking time to listen, linger, wonder and speculate.

On a wet winter walk, we find 'a stick what looks like antlers' and 'a piece of the moon' (conker shell). Lots and lots of sticks, leaves and grass are secreted in pockets. Many tiny, striped snail shells seem at first to be all the same but actually 'they are all different and beautiful'. We bring our treasures back and share our thoughts and memories. The objects represent other things, real and imaginary. We recall walks with our families and things we've found before. We find a discarded beach ball: 'I think there's a beach nearby. Maybe it's a secret beach'.

All our special sticks are collected together in the classroom. The children share their ideas with each other about what the sticks can represent: 'sticks

101

are lovely' and they can become 'antlers – a deer's hat', 'a pretend fishing rod', 'rockets' and 'a rainbow'. The children create new things with the sticks: a dream catcher, a picture frame, magic wands, swords and boats'. Everyone shares information and inspiration while we discuss the endless possibilities of the stick.

Another cold and muddy morning the children set off to find the secret beach. They have drawn a map [this is a frequent response in 5x5x5] 'so we know which way to go'. We catch the wind in plastic bags and call down the clouds that can take us to the secret beach. 'The cloud's called Holly and you have to shout for her'. We float leaf boats and a sledge for 'a teeny weeny elf' down a rainwater 'waterfall' in the road. Adding to our collections, we find a rusty tin 'that might be gold or jewels'.

The children and adults bring in their special things from home, objects they have found. We try to guess what some of them are: 'an olden day thing', 'a bit of a fallen-off wooden church'. We all listen carefully to each other's stories. 'We found it on holiday. First my daddy made it for my mummy. She wore the necklace all the time on holiday.' The children enjoy each other's memories and these prompt further recollections. They keep their things in 'special boxes' at home: 'I got a whole collection of this stuff.' Each object has a place on the big shared blue carpet and we photograph them all.

The children decide they want to share the story and their memories with others. They could 'turn all the classroom and playground into a museum', but instead they decide to 'make the museum in the wall on the terrace' [a rough country wall of huge stones]. They 'make a hole in the wall and dig it out and put the things inside' and, over three weeks, create a Museum of Found Objects that includes photographs of their special things and objects they make from the sticks and other things they have collected. Their museum is 'the best thing we've had ever' and the children decide to celebrate it with a grand opening for parents and siblings. It is a way of sharing an on-going fascination with collections and 'precious stuff' and its contents collect the children to their families and the world around them.

'You are seeing the inside of something when you see it with your heart,' says one of the children. 'You find out more and more.'

A version of this learning story appeared in Early Education Journal *54 Spring 2008*

b) Bishop Henderson Primary School
Annabelle Macfadyen and Sandy Shepard

The Nursery Class attached to Bishop Henderson Primary School in Coleford has been involved in 5x5x5=creativity for three years. Annabelle (artist) and Sandy (teacher) worked with a team of Nursery staff alongside parents and governors, who acted as observers and documenters. This is their story.

In the first sessions we observed the children's play and picked up on their enjoyment of physical expression and the way they communicated through their bodies. This inspired us to focus our research on their spontaneous movement.

Our initial provocation was to move the furniture and create a space in the classroom, a defined area where the children were free to move around in any way they chose. Adults joined the children in the space, responding to their

invitations to move with them, mirroring their movements, offering physical support and entering fully into their play. Materials such as mats, scarves, elastic rings, fabrics and also music were provided, and these extended the children's explorations.

As we observed and reflected on the movement, we tuned into children's preferences and ways of moving and expressing themselves. We also considered different theories and research to help us understand and analyse the children's movement.

Rebecca developed her movement vocabulary through her interaction with Annabelle (artist). Initially this was in the form of non-verbal greetings:

> Rebecca positions herself in front of Annabelle and makes eye contact. She raises her arms out to the sides and moves the top part of her body from side to side rhythmically whilst making quick, stepping movements with her feet.

Annabelle responded by mirroring Rebecca's non-verbal communications and over time these developed into a more complex series of movements. She became particularly interested in exploring balance, holding positions and perfecting bodily skills.

By experimenting with using an adult as a support to take her weight, she devised sequences of acrobatic movements. We could see Rebecca's confidence growing as she took risks and delighted in showing her movements to others.

We observed Henry developing his movement repertoire as a result of making relationships with particular individuals in the group. At first he remained outside the movement space and gradually approached the edge. When he first came in he stood still, observing the children and staying close to his friend. Henry developed a connection with Sandy (teacher) through movement games, physical interaction and use of materials.

Henry brings chiffon fabric and puts it over Sandy's head, while she is sitting on the floor. He places his hands gently on the sides of her head and moves his face closer, remaining still as they make eye contact and smile at each other through the fabric.

Through his developing relationship with a classmate, Billy, Henry began to be drawn into more flexible and free-flowing movements. Together they explored different pathways by weaving in and out, changing direction and stopping and starting. We noticed that Henry maintained a physical connection with Billy (holding hands or using materials) that we felt reflected their growing emotional bond and trust in each other.

During the sessions connection became a theme. The children increasingly chose to move together in pairs or groups, becoming more aware of each other and more cooperative. Their enjoyment and excitement grew as they took ownership of the space and there was a sense of the group operating as a community with its own culture and shared understandings. The children were both adventurous and sensitive in their movement explorations, developing their kinaesthetic awareness, and listening to and learning from their bodies.

As a way of helping the children to begin to reflect on their experiences, Annabelle gave short performances, incorporating the movements of children whom she had observed. The children responded with enthusiasm and a desire to be in the performance space themselves. They could thus become involved as creators, performers and audience. The experience of watching others also encouraged them to extend their personal movement vocabulary.

The team of adults came together after each session to reflect on what had been observed, share ideas and agree ways to follow and develop the children's interests. These in-depth discussions were often animated, inspiring and challenging, as different viewpoints were debated.

Our research into the ways children express themselves and communicate through their bodies gave us an insight into how important movement is in children's learning. Through close observation and moving with the children we were able to engage with their interests, curiosities, feelings, ideas and questions, which added another dimension to our understanding of them. When we tuned into this powerful form of communication we began to recognise how articulate children are in the language of movement and the value of giving our attention to and supporting their movement play.

c) The Big Square at Footprints Children's Centre
Lindsey Fuller

It was with great excitement and a little trepidation that we embarked on our learning journey as part of 5x5x5=creativity research with our two to four year-old children. How would we know what these two year-olds' real fascinations were? How would we respond to these in meaningful and creative ways? How would we really understand what we were seeing? We decided to focus on the children's non-verbal responses by observing their repeated patterns of behaviour or schemas and their levels of involvement, to help us to get to the heart of their thoughts and curiosities.

Our research began by observing the children. We noted that the exploration of monsters was deeply rooted in their play, and also the schemas of enveloping, containing, transporting and transformation. We decided to use these fascinations. As an initial provocation Helen, our artist, created an animated film about a monster, set in our nursery and incorporating these themes. We projected this film onto a large screen in the nursery to twenty children. They were immediately captivated.

Next we set up video cameras around the rooms and outside and played the film over and over again. We waited with baited breath for the children's many different responses: 'Where did it come from?' 'Where's it gone?' 'Do it again!' The children responded with surprise, amusement and delight.

Some children were puzzled and looked at the data projector and then back to the screen. Where were these images coming from? Others jumped up and went to look behind the screen, giggling and jumping back as the monster appeared. Other children pretended to feed the monster, snatching their hands away quickly to make sure they didn't get gobbled up.

Suddenly, Aleasha noticed the film had been recorded in her own nursery, 'It's there; it's the same as over there.' She pointed excitedly to the role play area and then back to the screen: 'It's the same!'

This prompted a hunt all over the nursery to find the monster. In the midst of this excitement an insistent voice was heard: 'I want to make him! I just want to make him!'

This first session sowed the seeds for the many different pathways the children explored. They were catapulted into an exploration of film making, model making, role play and transformation. We began to explore the concept of 'possibility thinking' as the children moved from 'What is this and what does it do?' to 'What can I do with it?' They became film makers, photographers, investigators and model makers. It was our role to provide an environment which nurtured and encouraged the endless possibilities coming from the children.

On reflection we realised that some children were more fascinated by the technology than by the film itself. But we wondered how much our two year olds would understand about their exploration into film making. We were amazed! How could we dare to doubt the tremendous capacity of these young children's minds?

The children returned again and again to the video cameras around the room, watching themselves on the viewfinder, capturing their friends and the monster they had found hidden in a drawer. They watched, fascinated, as the image in the viewfinder got larger or smaller. As the project progressed we observed the children deepening their understanding about cameras and filming and making more complex connections.

Issy was fascinated by the technology and quickly made the connection that the data projector somehow made the film appear. She moved the wheel that controlled the lens backwards and forwards. Was she wondering if her actions were making the images appear and change? She found the buttons on the data projector and Helen showed her the functions and she experimented with them. Her interest transferred to the video cameras and by the end of the project she was observed filming and directing a group of children and an adult:

> Issy moves camera.
> 'I'm going to see you Lindsey.'
> 'Stand back, go back.'
> 'Stand in the middle Lindsey.'
> 'Levi, go over there, next to the door.'
> 'I got you Lindsey.'

We began with the belief that children are strong and competent. As our research progressed this belief was confirmed by seeing the children demonstrate the tremendous capacities of their minds. They worked skilfully, making and experimenting with cameras and film making but they had not quite made the connection that many of the films we were watching were the ones they had made.

As adults we engaged in our own 'possibility thinking'. If we continued to enable the children to explore the world around them with cameras, would

Children re-viewing their film.

they make the leap in understanding from 'that's my model', to 'that's the film I made of my model'?

At Footprints we are striving to provide an environment that supports children in their exploration of their own inquires in many different creative languages. We want to encourage the children to push the boundaries to the very limits of their understanding and beyond. If we fail to do this, we are in danger of stunting the massive potential of our children.

d) Three Ways Special School
Lesley Hunt and Helen Jury

Working with learning difficulties brings its own catalogue of variables: differing cognitive and physical abilities, varying levels of concentration and internalisation of ideas. Some children do not vocalise. Fantasy is not necessarily followed through, narrative is not always developed and group play is sometimes hard for the children to sustain. It can also mean that various themes develop at the same time, and may as quickly be lost, neglected, or taken up once more. However, the sessions offered by 5x5x5 have allowed us to document the impetus caused by creative provocation manifested over a period of time.

With the theme of enclosure, Aiden (age 4) had returned to what he thought was 'the big box', only to find it was now flat – it had been squashed. This made him 'sad', which he demonstrated to all around him. However, he decided that he wanted it to remain flat and referred to this 'flat box' as 'the monster'. Were Aiden and Helen scared of the 'flat box monster'? It was suggested that it could have eyes and legs, and Aiden now wanted it to have a big belly – 'Bigger! Bigger! BIGGER!' And toes and teeth too. Aiden then asked for it to have wings so that it could fly. These were then cut out and put on the 'Big-Flat-Belly-Monster'.

Aiden and Ash (age 5) now became scared and hid inside the den and in the big box. They came out and watched as the Big Flat Belly Monster's shape was cut out, and then hid once more as Chloe (age 5) was eaten up by the 'BFBM'. She didn't appear to mind, but it was thrilling for Aiden and Ash. They became a little braver and blew raspberries at the BFBM, which made it become frightened of them in turn, so that it folded into itself and went away. Ash and Aiden were sad at this and decided to leave the room.

When they returned, the BFBM had been suspended from a line across the room, along with images of some of the children on an acetate window. We wanted to see if this promoted recognition amongst the group of each other and of the BFBM. Now however, the cardboard monster seemed to stimulate little response. The development of the group, and interactive role playing were being promoted and documented, and it was decided to make the BFBM more 'real' to see if it provoked a reaction from the children.

So the monster was placed inside the den and peered out of one of the makeshift windows, allowing the children to discover it and to find it ready to participate in their narrative as the BFBM character once more, or be incorporated

113

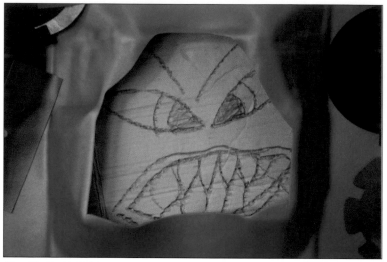

The Big Flat Belly Monster.

and developed in their play as they may choose in some other way. The acetate sheet window of images remained suspended, and other cardboard boxes were supplied for the children to elaborate on the enclosure theme in case they wished to develop this too. Aiden recognised the image of the BFBM on the acetate window and asked 'where monster?' When pointed in the direction of the den, he immediately engaged in role play, roaring fiercely and throwing boxes at it to prove who was stronger and fiercer, thereby beginning to construct a narrative around the character. He communicated his ideas to Helen, saying that the monster was coming, asking for it to be taken from the den, and saying that it could fly: 'Fly! Fly! Fly!' while taking it up and throwing it into the air to test his theory.

Soon the wings, attached by butterfly clips so they could flap, came off. This upset Aiden, but he began to develop the role-play further, asking for the wings to be put on *him*. Holes were made in the wings and Aiden put them on, then took them off and tried to attach them to the den and then to block the tunnel leading to the den's entrance. He put them back on and chased Libby (age 5), roaring at her in a suitably BFBM way. However, he became disgruntled by how the wings wouldn't stay on and asked Helen to fix them on better. They were tied on with string and then Aiden went to the mirror and studied his new apparel, from the front, back and sides. He chased the other children roaring again, becoming the monster himself.

When Aiden moved on to other play, he abandoned the wings. They were taken up by Libby, who coloured them with pastels and chalks and then put

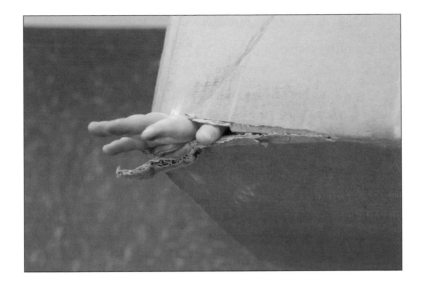

them along the foam rubber shapes she had put on over her head. When she, too, abandoned them to go to play in the den with Aiden, they were forgotten. However, Callum (age 6) pulled down netting covering the den and tried to put it over Helen and then, attracted to the drawn face of the BFBM, began to cover this too. He spent a long time simply sitting and studying the face of the monster while the other children played around him.

Melissa's (age 6) interaction with Aiden generated an on-going narrative. Together they played in the den which Melissa likened to a 'tree-house', hiding from the BFBM, which became a 'ghost'. They moved house from the den to a large cardboard box, which had the home comforts of a make-believe quilt and pillow. Smaller boxes were used to seal themselves inside. Aiden then got into the box and developed his own 'big tummy', similar to the BFBM. A drawing was made of Aiden and his tummy, but Melissa responded 'That's not Aiden!' and promptly drew a large 'Aiden Monster'. Aiden then drew his version – mostly over Melissa's. Helen cut out the picture and this became another monster, which nibbled their fingers when they poked them through the narrow slits in their box-home. Together they developed this theme by feeding the new BFBM, taking some sticky strips and rubber stickers to stick onto the BFBM's tummy to feed it and to fill it up. Hands were drawn and coloured in, 'fed' into the new BFBM's tummy. This was so that it wouldn't feed on any more fingers poking out of boxes – now they were safe.

LINES OF ENQUIRY

a) Learning dispositions

Susi Bancroft, Mary Fawcett and Penny Hay

5x5x5=creativity research emerges from the real experiences, exchanges and interests of the participants. Evaluation stresses the 'illuminating' nature of the work. By revealing and sharing learning together we seek to make meaning from our own work and then to link and extend our thinking through reference to current research.

During 2004 we began to frame a consistent area of long-term enquiry, discussion and interest about 'learning dispositions'. We had discovered that many participants wanted to research children's attitudes to learning and behaviours towards learning. We needed to create a shared language – ways of talking about these together – and look for any hypotheses, patterns and consistencies we could research further. From their experience of the Creative Foundation project, Sightlines Initiative suggested we focus on what children

were making of their experiences and how they responded. They identified six areas of behaviour – engagement, curiosity, communication, theories, exchanges and learning dispositions.

To support and stimulate thinking we offered professional development, some linked reading and possible tasks. The range of material included:

- Csikszentmihayli (1998) about the state of 'flow'

- Laevers (1994) about levels of involvement

- Eskesen (notes from Denmark in 2003) about what needs children have in order to learn

- Te Whaariki – New Zealand's curriculum strands of well-being, belonging, contribution, communication and exploration

- Claxton and Carr (2004) about the dynamics of learning dispositions and the environments that support them.

We believe that children want to learn, and it is our responsibility to encourage this desire in varied and complex situations. We want them to feel they belong, to engage and to achieve for themselves as a lifelong learners in many environments.

In learning to be learners we need to pay attention to attitudes, values, and developing habits of mind towards learning. This key understanding has ultimately led us in 5x5x5 towards our four current areas of research: creative values, creative dispositions, creative environments and creative relationships. We have amassed quantities of evidence during the research that shows children engaged in rich and deep ways. It was not only the content of their learning we noticed but the way in which they were learning: their persistence, concentration, motivation, curiosity, connection-making and collaborative ability. The astonishment and excitement of the adults at the children's sophistication in these respects drove us to look further and deeper. Our research has therefore concentrated on what lies beneath the surface – through careful observation, documentation and reflection we have investigated much deeper learning.

There is no single agreed set of dispositions and this makes the contribution of 5x5x5 important in this field. We determined to use our own evidence, grounded in observation, to draw together some collective definitions.

Our first collection was organised into areas as values, capacities, behaviours and dispositions, from which we tried to refine concepts. From our col-

leagues' feedback we were able to discuss and differentiate these conceptual qualities.

The next stage was to ask colleagues to collect learning stories that demonstrated one or two dispositions such as perseverance or willingness to explore. Over time, this became a natural part of 5x5x5 work and discussion, similar to that of noticing schemas when looking at children's play, fascinations and interests.

By 2005 we could refine our colleagues' discussion of their observations of the children to be concerned with:

- willingness to become involved
- playfulness and imagination
- self-propulsion, confidence in themselves as a learner
- perseverance, keeping involved
- resourcefulness, ingenuity
- collaboration, sharing ideas
- enquiring, being curious

- making connections
- concentration, sustained involvement.

Showing curiosity, a willingness to explore and to hypothesise, to think of new possibilities and make connections characterise the quality of learning in 5x5x5 settings.

> Curiosity and the exploratory drive: a lot of effort within the area of education is content based. That explains why, generally, the disposition of curiosity or, in a broader sense, the exploratory drive, doesn't get as much attention as it deserves. Investing in the preservation or even, strengthening of the exploratory drive can be seen as most rewarding in so far as it guarantees lifelong learning. An exploratory attitude, defined by openness for, and alertness to, the wide variety of stimuli that form our surroundings, makes a person accessible, lowers the threshold for getting into a state of 'arousal' [flow] that brings a person into the most intense forms of concentration and involvement. That person will never stop developing. The challenge for education is not only to keep this intrinsic source of motivation alive, but also to make it encompass all domains that belong to reality. (Laevers, 2000a)

In 2007 we tried to re-evaluate how the staff and artists in the settings had observed and documented the learning dispositions of the children. Participants now not only share a common language, but use this confidently and fluently. They choose words or terms for building up their own lists of interesting dispositions and looking for progression and depth within them.

The current evidence of learning dispositions shows children learning to be creative learners and developing long-lasting habits of mind. We recognise the danger in simply making lists, as it could become a kind of prescription of 'things to look for'. As with many aspects of this subtle research, it is the experience of engagement – observing and documenting children in real situations with open minded attentiveness that offers up these dispositions and behaviours in abundance for us to reflect on.

Two examples will convey the flavour of colleagues' observations. The first is Urchfont Preschool's observations of their music sessions in 2007, which resulted in the following evaluation of learning qualities in children:

> Prediction, persistence, focus, confidence, playfulness, imagination, collaboration, willingness to be involved, making connections, experimenting, concentration, enquiring, being curious, independence, initiating their own ideas. (Bancroft *et al*, 2007)

When asked what she had observed Charlotte (educator at Margaret Stancomb Nursery and Infant School) replied

> Loads. Resilience. Better interpersonal skills, more relaxed. Problem solving. Valuing each other's work, social skills and negotiation skills – some lovely working collaboratively. Involvement levels huge (reaching level 5 of Laevers' scales of involvement). Ability to deal with conflicts and difficulties.(*ibid*)

b) Fantasy play
Susi Bancroft

> ... if you truly allow children the freedom to play and explore in a safe and stimulating setting, then many/most will naturally use fantasy role play as their chosen medium. Their sure-footedness in negotiating the path between reality and a fluently improvised invented narrative demonstrates how natural this state of existence is for them. (Harker in Bancroft *et al*, 2005)

In this section we consider some general aspects of fantasy play and conclude with some examples.

For children aged between 3 and 7 fantasy play is the natural realm, one they draw us back to time after time. The child has the greatest authority in this form of play and it is where adults must enter sensitively and with integrity.

Children have the ability to move seamlessly between reality and fantasy interweaving themes they seem to share intuitively.

These themes are powerful and deep and include:

- relationships and roles such as parent, sibling, babies and friendship
- loss and being lost
- care and nurture
- identity
- fears
- aspirations
- superheroes and created figures who re-enact known and newly invented scenarios
- people, places and creatures both known and fantastic.

5x5x5 deliberately involves artists with strong expertise to support and maximise potential for fantasy play. These artists are able to cross the fantasy/reality borders unselfconsciously, and with integrity. Everyone who is involved allows themselves to be fully submerged in the play or in documenting it and not distracted by self-consciousness. The adults are following the children's lead and the fascination of their seemingly quicksilver movement through themes and scenarios. Children of this age move fluently in and out of fantasy to do such things as check detail, negotiate, diffuse the intensity of the situation.

They can re-enter the same play with long time gaps and pauses and recall and resume fast-flowing action with passion, concentration and great commitment. It is a world which children know they own. They have rules, language and patterns of behaviour which are child-led and there is no doubt or uncertainty about who is in charge! However, children revel joyfully in appropriate adult involvement and stimulus and in taking on their skills or suggestions. They are also good at ignoring or rejecting them when they are inappropriate, with a confidence rarely seen in other activities. They accept, reject, use elements and intertwine with a logic and purpose which is unquestionably surefooted and requires and elicits respect from those working with them. It is a space where it is an honour to be included as an adult.

The opportunities arise for close research into children's thinking as the fantasy realm and story making process provide rich and fertile ground for developing our understanding of children's 'philosophical thinking, questioning, collaborative ability, emerging views, analytical thinking and logic, emotional concerns, interests, preoccupations and creativity' (Bancroft, 2006).

The approaches in 5x5x5 practice are varied. At Freshford School the artists followed through the emergence of a collaborative fantasy play about bears, which arose from the provocation of a walk outdoors during which the strong engagement with a sense of place led to the discovery of a 'bear's hideout' and of fur and footprints. The children kept this fantasy theme alive throughout, generating energy to sustain and share it with interested adults. Parallel work on map-making enabled their interests to intertwine and extend.

124

'You may not be able to see the bears, but I can,' declared Beth. This powerful statement from a child acknowledges the nature of fantasy: the invitation to be included and to prolong the play, to imagine, to know the reality boundaries that provide safety when intensely engaged. The children engaged with the ideas at a level of disbelief with which they felt comfortable, closely observed by mindful adults. The adults shared their thinking about handling strong emotions and fears. One child, Iain, talked about the extra pair of 'sensors' he used to tell him when something scary was about to happen and which afforded him protective covering. Issues of fantasy and suspension of disbelief differ culturally within families, so the parents were involved and informed and could support their children (Bancroft *et al*, 2000).

St Saviour's School began one year with the line of enquiry: 'What is make-believe?' The school worked from a story they felt was 'a transformative catalyst, [that] draws you in, creates a mental landscape, [and where] objects become charged with significance' (Harker in Bancroft *et al*, 2005).

The story was a backbone or platform to build on. St Saviour's used drama games, story work and a workshop structure. The artist felt that the nature of the play required her to be 'totally involved, in the flow and immersed with the children'. Self-consciousness would have prevented the free flow of sustaining the children's threads of thinking. A documenter recorded what took place – essential for later discussion, reflection and enquiry.

A very different approach to fantasy was observed at Hollyhocks Kindergarten where Rachel, the artist, was a dance and movement specialist. After becoming acquainted with the children over a few weeks, she transformed the space – a village hall. The room was dimmed by drawing the curtains. Hanging across the middle of the room was a large muslin screen onto which blue light was projected. An atmosphere was created through carefully chosen music, to evoke the sea and water. A few props, resources for drawing and an overhead projector were made available.

The children entered the space with a quietness, an intensity of concentration. Rachel said nothing but moved gently to the music. Soon most of the children joined her. She encouraged them to watch their shadows, which were projected onto the large muslin curtain. Then she began imitating their movements and the children in turn played at imitating each other. Most of this was non-verbal. Then quite quickly an idea was sparked: 'we're sharks chasing mermaids'. This continued into an extended improvisation. The children sought out the props – cushions and rugs – and built underwater castles. It seemed that the play could continue for ever. Boys and girls were equally involved, al though a few children spent most of their time drawing. The staff wondered how parents would react to a similar light experience (see chapter 5 on parent participation).

At Four Acres Nursery, Travelling Light Theatre Company used the staging of the story *Clown* by Quentin Blake to make an installation. It was later transported to the theatre as part of the production and to stimulate story making.

The artist Sandra led the children through the story of *Clown* using mime and no speech. The children were richly engaged.

Later Vivian Gussin Paley's story square was used as a structure for encouraging and developing the children's ability to make stories and for modelling skills about story structure and dramatic presentation for the teachers. 'Stories were told all over the room and the children filled the air with performance'. The children displayed a sophisticated and sustained capacity to make stories and share them. Speaking and listening skills blossomed, and so

did the love of stories and a desire to share and communicate them. Skills that are so essential to later learning emerged naturally and were nurtured. One child approached an adult 'with her fist clenched, saying 'I've got a story in my hand and I need to get it out!' (Bancroft *et al*, 2005).

Props often serve as supports or provocations and work best when they are open-ended and flexible. Children in the early years move easily between different types of play using 'multi-modal' ability (Kress in Anning and Ring, 2004). We have many observations of children expressing their imaginative ideas through a mixture of playful learning modes, such as narrative role play, music, drawing or making. They move fluently between these modes, picking them up and discarding them as their play develops.

Fantasy play and story making can be emotionally tense, noisy, physical – and it requires space. 5x5x5 respects the time, space and attention this natural and effective play demands. Documenting the children's imagination and learning and then discussing and reflecting on it and extending possibilities gives insights into children's thinking and extends our understanding.

This natural learning medium is richly productive. Children are always ready to instigate and deepen their involvement. The trying out of ideas, free association and creative connections evoke sustained concentration, collaboration, resourcefulness and passion – exciting ingredients for 'researching children researching the world'.

c) The outdoors
Liz Elders and Mary Fawcett

> I sincerely believe that for the child, and for the parent seeking to guide him, it is not half so important to know as to feel. If facts are the seeds that later produce knowledge and wisdom, then the emotions and the impressions of the senses are the fertile soil in which seeds must grow. The years of childhood are the time to prepare the soil. Once emotions have been aroused – a sense of the beautiful, the excitement of the new and the unknown, a feeling of sympathy, pity, admiration or love – then we wish for knowledge about the object of our emotional response. Once found it has lasting meaning. It is more important to pave the way for the child to want to know than to put him on a diet of facts he is not ready to assimilate. (Carson, 1998)

At least two thirds of 5x5x5 settings have been attracted to the outdoor environment as the place for their research. Why is there a strong pull from

both children and adults towards working outside? What are the reasons why so many have chosen to make this decision? The triangles began with different motivations but as time went on perspectives have developed and we will review these.

Practicalities

Most of the settings do not have an *atelier*, a workshop, or even a designated space which can be used for 5x5x5 work. Many classrooms are small and the hall may be constantly in demand. Using outside areas on the school sites where there is no pressure on time and sufficient open space has proved a practical and logical choice in several schools. Some settings have taken eagerly to regular walks in natural areas. The extra numbers of adults in a 5x5x5 session helps to meet adult/child ratio requirements.

A context for exploration

Finding a space is clearly important but the decision runs deeper than this. Wild spaces are ideal for exploring the unstructured world. In St Saviour's conservation area the staff focused on make-believe. For the children the area became a separate world which they inhabited in their own ways. Regardless of the weather they were out there, making full use of bushes to hide behind, a pond to 'fish' in, trees to climb, space to dig, etc. (see St Saviour's case study). Outdoors is a natural realm for exploring the world.

Discovering children's real motivations

Taking an initial walk, whether in urban or rural neighbourhoods, provides a rich context for the purpose of discovering children's schemas and interests. Away from the classroom and the curriculum agenda children can reveal their true selves. Since 5x5x5 is child-led, the adults can observe and discover children's fascinations by documenting an initial exploratory walk. This makes a good starting point. The adults involved also have a sense of freedom – a feeling of being removed from the structured educational environment and the planned curriculum. Fresh thinking can be liberated. The situation seems to grant permission for a different kind of approach and opportunities for creative possibilities. Notably, when adults are challenged in professional development sessions to identify personal childhood creative experiences, most of the examples they give are located in outdoor environments.

As a conceptual enquiry

Tabitha's reflection on bringing the outside in and taking the inside out at the Kinder Garden led to philosophical debate by children and adults about the

concept of what makes the outside different from inside and what qualities each holds. They engaged in many walks in the neighbourhood parks and gardens and the children as well as the adults took photographs. In the nursery garden, the children took part in designing a structure constructed by the artist and her colleagues which could be used as a castle or a spaceship, or whatever the children decided. Inside they even turfed the classroom to create the outside inside, as the children wanted (see Kinder Garden case study page 69).

A local community resource

At First Steps the new nursery found a treasure on their doorstep: Carr's Wood. It proved a wonderful regular environment for the children and adults to immerse themselves in the possibilities of fields, woods, and stream. Would the children be most interested in the micro-world of mini-beasts or the macro-world of adventurous space? To start with it was the sticks and mud which were the predominant interests. However, later mini-beasts became a fascination. The staff were anxious to offer nursery children a genuine natural environment since so many live in flats or have unsuitable gardens, some with discarded syringes lying about. Many parents were unfamiliar with this local wild space and enjoyed our exploring it together. The practicalities of suitable all-weather outdoor gear for the children were resolved by providing over-trousers and boots. The challenge of documenting with very active children in the rain and wind was managed by using a camcorder.

We found that when given an agenda which favours exploration children seem to continue their play indefinitely and with absorbed concentration. As one child said on arriving in a well designed park area 'We could play here for hours!' And they did!

As we saw in our consideration of the creative and reflective cycle, children in the group may draw on different modes of enquiry and expression. Take Cameron, who looked at a huge partially cut-down tree and mused 'This is dinosaur land. Before my Mummy and Daddy were here there was a battle between Tyrannosaurus Rex and Diplodocus and they broke the tree.'

Adults seem to have a strong urge to correct children's theories and are anxious about allowing them to formulate 'wrong' hypotheses when these refer to a body of knowledge like science. Mentor Liz notes that science depends on curiosity, observations, hypotheses, testing out and deductions. Children do all these in their explorations. They do learn facts, but facts can be subject to change. More important in education is to model the processes of learning. She suggests we need to avoid the temptation simply to label, for example, 'a leaf' but rather to model attention to the colours, shape, veins, texture and more.

Revisiting an area tends to trigger similar stories, collections and experiments. In one case the clay in a stream led to making monsters and later to creating a family of monsters. The following week they made a club house for the monsters at the top of the path.

The unstructured outdoors is wonderfully rich in possibilities for children to be scientists, builders, collectors, historians, explorers, storytellers, scene designers, artists. It is a richly textured learning environment – a place where all modes of learning are possible and can flourish in a different, extended and complementary way to learning indoors (see Austin, 2007).

The benefits of being outside

The benefits of being outside are legion, as our research has shown. The experience of wild spaces is rarer for children than we expected. Some became anxious and kept very close to the adults at first, checking them for signals as to what they might do. In some settings it is necessary to find funding for suitable clothing such as wellies. But extending the children's experience of the world into the horizon of the outdoors is of immense benefit.

Colleagues in 5x5x5 are constantly reflecting on and adding to our understanding of the benefits of being and learning outdoors. We made the following informal collective list of suggestions about what it offers:

- a chance for greater freedom, making more noise and larger movements

- playing freely with natural materials which the adults don't have to be too controlled about

- learning what is living and what not e.g. that it is appropriate to cut off wood the tree 'no longer needs'

- learning about creatures and plants

- following the seasons, the changes in growth, flowers, leaves, temperature

- experiencing weather, the rain on your face. Nursery age Billy, all on his own, was observed peacefully looking up into the high branches of huge beech trees, smiling and singing to himself as the rain dripped on his face

- physically developing skills of walking on awkward terrain, climbing

- becoming self-confident and self-sufficient, using their initiative

- playing and exploring

- observation skills, noticing changes on both a macro and micro scale

- understanding the environment, how one thing affects another

- listening to outdoor sounds

- benefiting physically from fresh air and free movement

- a rich context for role play

- using their imagination.

From our reading we would add that taking children into open spaces also provides:

- opportunities to express emotions

- gaining control over minds and muscles

- meeting the need for risky freedom

- experiencing things that only happen outside

- motivation and physical engagement

- improved behaviour, being active should not be perceived as being a problem in childhood, it is necessary

- the outdoors especially serves the particular documented needs of boys

- an essential environment for learning and teaching.

> ... if we believe that young children learn through play – that play is thought in action – then offering children playing space outdoors would seem the most efficient means to fulfil their need to play, learn through first-hand experiences and co-operate with others. [Ouvry also emphasises the value of risk taking because] Being at the edge of what they can manage is where learning happens. It is when the environment that we set up for children enables them to be adventurous and show physical and social courage that children can begin to understand themselves and others. (Ouvry, 2000)

The environment is the third teacher, according to educators in Reggio Emilia. It develops generic concepts of space, context, culture, time and change as well as specifically offering children both solitude and community, and developing aesthetic sensibility.

d) Musical intelligences
Mandy Adams and Mary Fawcett

Context

By musical intelligences we mean the many elements of understanding the world of sound and music. Music is a language all of its own. To quote musician Chartwell Dutiro: 'The moment we start playing music, language doesn't matter. The language is the music.' Music has at its heart different forms of expression and communication which include singing, movement and playing music on instruments. It also has its own vocabulary to describe the qualities of music such as pitch, timbre, rhythm, melody and tempo. Most of us are affected by the moods it can create as an expressive language and experience. We can feel deeply involved individually or as part of a group, dancing, singing or playing. And music is written down using various systems of notation in order to communicate it to others.

Music provides unique experiences, such as singing alone or with others, listening in a musical way, making sounds with objects in the environment, organising sounds, exploring the potential of musical instruments.

In 5x5x5 we have explored many of these qualities over the years. Musicians from a variety of musical traditions, introduced to us through our partnership with Womad Foundation, have worked in several settings. Children have experienced many types of instruments, from percussion such as drums, wood and metal sounds to shakers, and the *mbira* from Zimbabwe, and songs of all kinds. (Young and Glover, 1998 offer a wealth of information and sources of instruments.)

Maintaining our principles is a priority, in particular recognising the child's own approaches to music.

> We need to learn how to listen, to recognise and value young children's own ways of being musical and to see starting points for adults to connect with, follow and respond to. In contrast to other areas of early years practice, particularly the visual and language arts, I consider music lags behind in its collection, analysis and interpretation of young children's self-initiated activity. As a consequence, adult-led models of music practice dominate which are often, in my view, poorly connected with children's current abilities, competences and inclinations. (Young, 2003)

Young's philosophy and research is completely in tune with that of 5x5x5= creativity and her work has provided valuable insights into, and practical understanding of, the approach.

Netsai Chigwendere plays mbira.

Discoveries and questions

Thoughts from the evaluation interview of Joanna, musician, and Rebecca, teacher, give insights into their nursery class experience:

They rated children's choice as a priority. The musical sessions were based on the children's interests and ideas and they involved active listening, valuing individuality and the process of learning. The adults allowed access to a wide range of resources including musical instruments, a CD player and CDs, and coloured scarves for moving to music with.

Joanna said she tried to encourage the children to think and talk about what they were doing. 'They find this difficult because there is a gap in children's musical vocabulary and musical experiences which limits their ability to express themselves verbally or through action.' Rebecca added that children can generally express themselves with familiar activities but found it harder with the musical activities.

Both musician and teacher agree that it has been a challenge to try and follow the children's ideas, for example when it gets too noisy. There is a balance between letting them work freely and deciding when it is enough.

The organisation of space was an important consideration. They decided to devote a corner of the room to music. This worked well as it wasn't in the flow

of traffic yet was still accessible to the children. 'It was important that the children were in a familiar environment so we didn't want to move to another room.' This type of organisation also works well with older children. However the sound can be disturbing to others in the room and what the rest of the children are doing can be distracting to the music group. The children need to have the freedom to move in and join the group, or move out of it.

Joanna noted that it was less distracting if there was not too much equipment out in the classroom. Offering too much at once can be chaotic.

> I have learnt how important the environment is and how it can influence the activity in either a positive or negative way.

> I have learnt not to try to get everyone involved all the time, particularly with this age range. They are engaged for different lengths of time. The most creative experiences have happened when I have been working one-to-one with a child or in a very small group. It has been good to have had the opportunity to work for a long time with individual children.

> No matter how much I want to step in I am now thinking about how I can stand back and still extend what is going on.

Certain learning dispositions were observed in the children over the year: predicting, persistence, focus, confidence, playfulness, imagination, collaboration, willingness to be involved, making connections, experimenting, concentration, enquiring and being curious, independent, initiating their own ideas. Music is particularly rich in possibilities and has a strong emotional impact. In documenting the 5x5x5 work, the adults concluded that 'the video has been fab for reflection and the photos have reminded us about what has been happening.'

Another 5x5x5 class who worked with Joanna visited the show *In one ear* at the egg children's theatre after they completed the sessions in school. The show proved to be just right for the age group: a well judged mix of humour, action, subtle story, sounds, shapes and music. The intense concentration of every child was remarkable. Their absorption in the mood – engaging but never overwhelming – and participation in the musical experiences was magical.

> ... as they were leaving I smiled to Toby, who knows me slightly, and he spontaneously said, with eyes wide and smiling from ear to ear, 'It was the loveliest thing that me and Daniel have ever been to'. (Mary, mentor)

The children were asked what they enjoyed most about Joanna coming in to school. Oliver replied that: 'she made me happy and sang lots of songs and got me lots of musical instruments.' He appreciated having fresh people in school: 'I liked it when she first came – it was great fun and she's new and 'cos you don't know who they are.' Oscar 'just liked the music: the sounds and the beat'.

Conclusion

Practical issues such providing a sufficiently peaceful environment and a small focus group seemed to be conducive to thoughtful experiences.

Colleagues identified a number of research questions they would like to address in the future:

- What are the differences between the visual arts and the sound arts?
- How best can we use music in a creative and non-directive way?
- To what extent should the musician use his or her musicianship?
- Might there be a difference between a musician and a workshop leader?
- What forms of preparation are needed for 'new' creative enablers so that they can join in established 5x5x5 groups?
- Relationships are important and take time to develop: what are appropriate time-scales for such work?
- How can music technology enrich the musical experiences of pre-school children, and be made more accessible to them?

e) Creative digital technologies
Liz Elders, Mary Fawcett, Lindsey Fuller and Ed Harker

5x5x5=creativity is part of a revolution in digital photography. At the start, seven years ago, everyone was taking photographs with cameras and film, hurrying off to get them processed, waiting patiently to collect them and then finding the few images of use. Now virtually everyone has a digital camera and their skills in using it, along with computers including Apple Macs, have developed exponentially.

The skills related to these digital technologies are a new kind of literacy, another language. But are there any contradictions or dilemmas arising from the new technologies? Are some people excluded because they cannot afford the equipment or lack the relevant skills? Do such tools move children too soon from the natural world to a technical one? Can this new literacy be incorporated into practice so that all the 5x5x5 principles are maintained? Other questions may also arise.

We have identified several areas where colleagues have used digital cameras to benefit and strengthen everyone's creative capacities and the qualities of our documentation. The areas discussed here are:

- documentation as both 'deep documentation' and a 'gallery of learning'
- research and professional development
- children's use of the technologies
- artists' innovative creative work

Deep documentation
The detail of documentation is referred to throughout this book. Here we note how the new technologies are of assistance. Gardner's phrase 'deep documentation' (in Giudici *et al*, 2001) refers to the use observations for reflection with both the children and adults in their joint constructions of meaning, thus going much deeper than typical classroom observations. Digital cameras have allowed for a sophisticated and deep process of reflection. They enable more material to be filmed and for far more selection. Colleagues can produce almost instantaneous material for discussion with the children.

Graphics tablets enable comments and annotations to be handwritten or drawn directly onto digital photos and images that have been inserted into a

PowerPoint presentation. This is especially powerful in the way that it allows the children to represent their ideas with photos taken only minutes before. Because the annotations can be saved, they can be revisited later, allowing layers of commentary and reflection to build up around a single image.

A gallery of learning
Creating material for sharing with parents, colleagues and other professionals is now easy. By running several display screens off a single computer, digital media can be shared beyond the classroom or setting. An extra screen can be placed against an external window, so that children and parents can view slideshows of photographs, film clips and other digital presentations. This is especially effective for documentation that has a strong narrative element.

Research and professional development

Everyone in 5x5x5 is engaged in the research process and documentation is the key source of material evidence. Colleagues bring their laptops to professional development sessions and regularly use PowerPoint to facilitate sharing their material with colleagues, at staff meetings and parent meetings. Access to sharing learning is fresh and lively.

Children's use of creative technologies

Liz (teacher) and Deborah (artist) report on their experiences:

> The children at the Kinder Garden had an emerging interest in pattern and symmetry and were exploring the placing and arranging of natural materials. In order to support this Andy Kemp, artist/photographer, introduced lens technology to the children. He set up a video camera linked live to a TV monitor. The video camera had the facility to split the screen image and mirror it, so producing a symmetrical image on the TV. (see page 139)

The following year a group of children aged 3-4 were sharing their interest in the Superhero film genre and a group of boys were trying out stunt actions in their Superhero role play. We introduced a video camera with a link to a live TV screen into the play area and wondered how it might affect their physical expressiveness. While trying out stunts, now in 'slow motion', to camera, they commented on being 'in' or 'out' of the film.

Some of the children wanted to be cameramen or directors as well as stunt actors. One boy expressed his dilemma: 'I can't work out how to be behind the camera and in front of it at the same time.'

We extended the use of the lens technology so they could express their ideas in other 'languages'. We wanted them to be able to view their physical movements as if frozen in time. A digital SLR (single lens reflex) camera was used to photograph their expressive movements with multiple frames per second. The printed sequences of photos fascinated the children. The girls began exploring a parallel theme of good versus evil through ballet (see page 121).

Some of the children went on to photograph their own action sequences using action figures to create their own animated sequences. They set up each frame, photographed it and then repositioned the figures for the next shot in their story.

The adults were intrigued by the effect the visual technology had on the children's expressive behaviour. Their role play and dance had a new quality which Deborah described as 'performic', meaning the children showed an awareness of audience – of audiences of both educators and parents.

Liz noticed other effects too. Through viewing themselves the children became more aware of their own movement and refinements of movements, more self-conscious. Movement was not just spontaneous and gone – it was as if they had acquired a deeper awareness of their own ability to express their ideas to themselves, as well as to audience.

> What you're describing is a central aspect of the practice of an artist. We do and then we look at what we've done, then we do some more with a new understanding and a sense of how it needs to be altered. It's a continuous process of action, re-viewing and refining that goes on over the years. The children, having instant access to visual representations of what they had just done, were immediately keen to see it; looked at it closely and then seemed to be spurred on to immediately repeat it with slight adjustments. Then they would want to view it again and so on. (Deborah)

Artists' innovative work

The artists are also experimenting with digital images, and work at Footprints Children's Centre has taken the possibilities further. Artist Helen chose as the first provocation for work with the children a series of animated films about a monster set in the nursery of two-year-olds. She created films incorporating the children's current interests and schematic play.

Educator Lindsey writes:

We projected these films onto a large screen in the nursery and left them running. The children then launched themselves into an exploration of film making. We set up video cameras around the Nursery for the children to explore. We were excited about how far we could push the boundaries of their understanding using this technology. Each week we were amazed at the boundless capacity of these young children's minds to understand complex concepts and ideas and use these to make their own investigations about film making. As adults we saw and used the rich possibilities of documenting using the filming we and the children had made.'

(For the full learning story from Footprints see page 110)

5

Perspectives on 5x5x5=creativity

a) Educators' perspectives
edited by Mary Fawcett and David Allinson

How does it feel to be involved in 5x5x5?

The interviews for the DVD provided useful insights into the 5x5x5 experience of teachers, who responded frankly and with humour. Annual reports also documented the educators' and teachers' insights and these contribute to this account.

The 5x5x5 structure, entailing regular collaboration by artist and educator, creates a 'completely new dynamic' (David, mentor). Practice becomes a shared responsibility, a sharp contrast for some teachers who say they generally feel very much alone inside their classroom walls.

> It provides the opportunity for joint thinking: artist and educator using each other as a sounding board, and in time, synthesising their thinking. New perspectives can challenge common, accepted practice which is sometimes hard to break away from due to the school culture or just lack of time to rethink. (David)

Some found partnership a challenge at first: 'I didn't know how it was going to work for me and with my nursery nurse and the artist' (Zoe). But many teachers talked enthusiastically about the benefit of fresh perspectives and impetus. Jayne appreciated how the artists bring 'a different way of working. They haven't got the educational baggage of systems and assessments.' The cultural centre contributed an additional element to the three-way collaborations, though not usually on a weekly basis in the classroom.

143

A striking view frequently expressed by the teachers is their perception of 5x5x5 as a new philosophy that 'starts from the children'. It is more accurate, though, to say that 'starting from the child' is a philosophy with a long tradition (see Doddington and Hilton, 2006). Everyone accepted the principle of observation and several spoke of 'learning to be quiet', but they found it difficult 'to sit back' and let go. For some it was hard to contain their enthusiasm 'when your own imagination is flying'.

Sam described the early stages as 'really uncomfortable, [I was] quite scared because you don't really know what is going to happen.' Zoe said that the beginning, when 'we were exploring and investigating was OK and exciting, but in the middle I thought, Where are we going? Why are we going this way?' Cathy's view was: 'You don't know what's going to happen. It's a project where you have to let go from day one and you don't do that as a teacher. I knew I had to be incredibly open-minded.'

As they spoke of their insecurity, it seemed that what most concerned them was the consequence of not having a pre-planned curriculum during 5x5x5 time – 'not having a weekly map or a daily timetable' – and the way their role changed from someone who controls most things to sharing the choice of direction with the children and the other adults. 'Should I be in there telling them what to do?' The uncertainty caused some to wonder whether they had the expertise and skills to meet the challenges: 'Where are the children going to take us? Are we going to keep up with the children?'

Others asked: 'Will I still be able to make the required assessments and will children make progress in the commonly assessed outcomes such as literacy and mathematics?'

They recognised that they had to think in terms of resources rather than themes and to 'think outside the box'. Lesley recognised that as a teacher 'you become set in your own ways. You develop your own style. 5x5x5 challenges the work you do.'

The 'edgy feelings' and uncertainty faded as the teachers began to 'follow the children's journeys'. Zoe talked about how she had never before taught this way, nor even had reception class children before, but by the end of the year she was speaking cheerfully about having been previously 'programmed' to do the National Curriculum and now 'I've had to re-programme myself. The children have helped me to do that.'

Anne, the headteacher, acknowledged how: 'you go deeper and deeper rather than wider and wider into understanding children's learning. It's a significant learning experience for us [the adults] too. You say to yourself: I wonder how I once learned about that.' Andrea (advisor) observed 'an astonishing level of dialogue, networking and sharing thinking. The adults had a much deeper understanding of learning.' One teacher described herself as an 'analyst now.'

Cathy was comfortable with the way her role had changed. At the start she had ideas about how the project would develop but the children moved the project on themselves.

> I have valued the opportunity to really observe for a good length of time. 5x5x5 enables me to sit back and watch and let the children go – allowing them to do the exploring and problem solving. They don't need an adult intervening every five minutes. You really get to know your children. It's about what I believe children should be doing on a daily basis. My job with the artist is a partnership – you feed off each other.

Another teacher said 'I've been a learner, I've learned to be quiet.'

The teachers' and artists' anxiety and uncertainty is taken seriously by the project team. 5x5x5 approaches this inevitable issue by having in place a multi-layered support framework. Professional development takes place on a one-to-one basis through the mentor support system, and in small groups through regular local authority group reviews, and more formal sessions for all 5x5x5 colleagues. Being part of a creative learning community where all have an equal voice enables people's confidence to grow.

Chris White summed up his interviews in 2007 with every Wiltshire teacher who had worked in 5x5x5 over the last two years:

> Some educators expressed an initial sense of obligation to plan and manage children's learning, regarding this as a part of their professional role and test of their competence. Often this practice was in conflict with their expressed values and beliefs that children should act with a good degree of freedom and agency ...The prospect of trying alternative approaches, trusting the children to develop their own controls and manage their own learning caused some anxiety [in the first year]. [In the second year] the weight of evidence and expectation had shifted, so that all assumed they would be adopting pedagogical practices in which they reduced their control over children's activities and gave more freedom and responsibility to the children. [An educator told me] '5x5x5 has allowed me to teach in the way I always wanted to'.

Other insights into the learning reported in the annual report (Bancroft *et al*, 2007) reveal the quality of the relationships between the adults. At Moorlands Infant School the educators and artist together responded with enthusiasm to a question about creative relationships: 'Dialogue! Endless chats! Recognising each other's roles and specialisms; the two different perspectives.'

145

> Our creative relationship was such that there was an unspoken mutual respect for each other's voices and a shared responsibility for documentation. We enjoyed working as a team in an atmosphere of laughter and enjoyment. We openly discussed problems and difficulties taking equal responsibility for overcoming them. (Educator, Freshford Primary School)

These quotes reflect two aspects of relationship building: interaction and the recognition of difference, expertise and perspective.

At Exeter House Special School the artist and educator dovetailed their observations and built on them. The longevity of 5x5x5 allows for a deepening of such possibilities. Here the artist and educator noted:

> knowing each other, our different styles of working and respecting each other's expertise through our previous collaboration had built up a trust, we could then freely bounce ideas off each other ... This enabled us to weave a whole tapestry as we responded to the children's interests and imagination.

David (mentor) writes:

> ... educators may question how practice 'within' 5x5x5 sessions impacts upon practice outside 5x5x5 sessions. How does it feel to be different within an establishment? Is it threatening or exciting? Do practitioners constantly feel a desire to 'spread the word'? The importance of support and acceptance of the whole school, including management colleagues cannot be overstated.

In sum, the teachers were sure that through 'observing very closely' they had learned about the children in their own class, about learning in general and their deepening personal learning. They now believe they understand about creative learning structures and processes.

> 5x5x5 has helped develop the staff's awareness of the importance of adults supporting the schematic development of each child by the use of skilfully facilitated child-initiated activities. We have been able to clarify the learning dispositions of the children more acutely; the outcome being that the learning has become more robust, resilient and meaningful. Needless to say, the above has significantly supported out behaviour management policy which is based on choice, consequence and democracy. (Headteacher Anne Forrest)

For further insights into the 5x5x5 experience see the DVD *100 voices* which features case studies involving all the speakers quoted here.

b) Parents' perspectives
edited by Mary Fawcett and Penny Hay

As 5x5x5 has progressed we have increased our engagement with parents and the local community. We have plenty of anecdotal evidence of parents being excited about connecting more with their children's learning, and understanding what the children have been telling them at home about their 5x5x5 experiences. Parents are becoming involved in many ways, coming in informally with objects of interest and telling staff about their children's continuing interest at home, as well as making more formal contributions. Every setting starts 5x5x5 work with a parents' meeting or coffee morning. Some organise workshops for parents and others create newsletters to share the children's learning stories. We have selected four examples of how parents have reacted to 5x5x5.

Parent documenters
Parents in many settings have taken responsibility for observing sessions. One parent documenter, Janice, spoke at our annual seminar about her experience.

How did I get involved?
I attended an introductory session for parents which told us about the project. We were asked if we would like to help and it so happened that I had recently been made redundant and had time to get involved. I was able to go along to sessions regularly and to take notes as documentation.

What did I enjoy?
I gained a great deal from my involvement. It was a pleasure being accepted by the children as one of the team. I enjoyed getting to know their individual characters. It was interesting to see how well they responded to the interest shown by the adults. Seeing my son Iain in his 'natural habitat', happy and confident, meant it was a very special time for us both.

What did I learn?
I learned how very different children are, how focused and industrious they can be and how they can co-operate, solve problems and organise themselves. I was struck by what a special age reception children are at: almost a transition between fantasy and fact. Being involved in the project in this way has had a very strong influence on the way I interact with my children and activities we do together. I would even go so far as to say it was a life-changing experience.

My feelings now about 5x5x5
My only problem with the project was that it took me a long time to get my head around what it was all about: I really only achieved this through seeing the work

evolve. I think that if it is to be successful, parents need to be helped to understand what it is all about. They need clear concise communication to see the benefits for their children; if not they could easily dismiss it as a waste of time.

The more my own understanding grew, the more benefits I could see and the more enthusiastic I became. I saw the children developing skills that I imagine would be difficult to teach in traditional ways. I could also observe their self-esteem growing.

In the future I would like all primary school children to have regular time-tabled sessions, possibly even something similar in secondary education. It would also be good to see science and engineering involved, as well as the arts. Finally in the words of my son Iain, 'That's the end with a full stop on the right!'

A workshop for parents

Hollyhocks Nursery offered parents a colour workshop. After the event Chrissie, leader of the preschool, wrote about her observations and reflections:

We put a lot of thought into preparing the space and the format of the session.

We decided to take the group on a journey through light, using three possible colours; white, blue, green and red. With flexibility of course!

We started the session with a darkened room, reflected white light, a large piece of muslin, white balloons, Esther playing her flute, and other team members playing the singing bowl, Tibetan bells, etc.

The team were all slightly apprehensive and nervous in a way that we wouldn't have been with a children's workshop. Why?

Possibly afraid of judgment and rejection.

Will anyone join in?

Suitability!

No real format – just ideas and resources.

Initially only one person turned up at the designated time, which felt very weird. Was anyone coming? Other people arrived in the next ten minutes; some looked a bit shell-shocked as they entered this unfamiliar space.

A couple were able to join in by finding a balloon or ribbon stick, others sat in the dark and watched.

There was some interaction by the brave ones. Two of the adults danced with the muslin, which acted as a trampoline for the balloons, someone started to roll under the cloth, and then delighted in being covered by it. Another stood very close to the screen, moving slowly, watching her shadow in the light. One parent had discovered the charcoal and began to draw, spiralling across the paper as if dancing in response to the music.

The words that came to mind to describe the atmosphere were 'haunting', 'magic', 'circus', 'surreal', and 'unpredictable'. There was no actual dialogue at all, but a lot of non-verbal communication through facial expression and body language and movement.

I was very conscious of and uneasy about so many adults sitting out. Surely it was fine for these people to sit out, were they happily watching and absorbing what was going on, or did they find it too hard to join in because they arrived late and thought they missed the beginning?

Did they think it was a load of rubbish and want to leave?

Why was it so difficult for me to ask them – was I afraid of what they might say? On reflection later, I realised that if this had been a group of children I would have sat with them for a while, given them the chance to comment on what they were observing and judge whether they were happy to stay watching or that they needed help or permission to join in.

After unsuccessfully engaging the adults on the sidelines, by way of balloons, etc. I communicated with Rachel (artist) and we decided to move up a gear, in the hope that a new phase might make it easier for them to participate.

Kathy projected running water and oil bubbles with inks onto the screen. (Someone later commented that this resembled a 1980s disco!) We changed the music to sounds of the sea and offered the large, stretchy blue cloth, which the children had loved. Would it entice more adults to join in?

The blue cloth evoked a more playful atmosphere, Rachel began to capture most of the adults who were sitting down by wrapping them up. And simply saying the words 'It's a cave' seemed to give them permission to join in. Did they feel safe and hidden in this space? Was this less scary than initiating their own play?

They began to move around the room *en masse* collecting others, directed by Rachel. At last there was some dialogue and laughter and a lot more physical interaction.

The leader's reflection

Personally I found this workshop both challenging and rewarding. It felt like a real risk and I was completely out of my comfort zone. But listening to people's reflections I realised how valuable an experience it had been for everyone and that the difficult moments were as valid as the relaxed playful ones. There were real similarities in the emotions evoked in the adults and children, but the children's play always contained characters and a narrative. Did the adults' inhibitions or lack of creative experiences hinder similar developments?

Under similar circumstances, the thing I would change in future is my belief in myself and I'd approach and support adults in the same way as I would the children, despite possible rejections.

Parents' reflections

Daunting; couldn't join in; hiding then revealing; self-conscious; safety in numbers; enticing; playful; calming; interesting to sit back and watch; going inside an enclosure provided safety; enjoyed the silence and non-verbal aspect; some people need words to join in; experience better – not just ready; freedom to do what you want; risky; peaceful; alternative; light and music important to set the scene; exploration; inclusion; invited in; I realised I never played as a child; feeling naughty – is this a good or bad feeling?, non-verbal communication, on entering space thought 'are we going to have a nice play?'

Two parents' responses to 5x5x5

An email to Penny

My son Cameron started at Malmesbury C of E Primary School, Wiltshire in September 2005 and has been fortunate enough to be involved in the 5x5x5 creative project, which he has found extremely enjoyable and during this time has made notable improvements in certain areas of his development.

This project has been excellent in motivating and encouraging the children to be creative and this process has, in my opinion, enhanced their overall development and motivation to learn.

During this project Cameron has been given the opportunity to explore and develop his own and other children's ideas in a creative environment that works alongside the usual educational requirements for this foundation year, and I can see how beneficial this has been to him. Children, particularly at this young age, naturally want to explore, learn and develop their skills and this project gives them the perfect opportunity to do so.

In the short time that Cameron has been involved in this project I have noticed distinct changes in his overall development. He is more creative, more confident, and better at problem solving. Cameron was fortunate in that he was also involved in the focus group with the artist Cathy Mills and this has led to major changes in the way he thinks, learns and acts. Cameron is creative and enjoys creative projects but this has taught him to develop his own ideas and he has, with no outside influence, started to work on projects of his own, one being a book which brings together not only the visual aspect of the project but also reading and writing skills which are a part of his general education. Cameron is not an overly confident child but working with Cathy and having to share ideas, voice opinions, and make suggestions has help him to be more confident in himself and his abilities.

Cameron has without a doubt enjoyed every aspect of the 5x5x5 project that he has been involved in and in my opinion the influence Cathy Mills and the project overall has had on him will be something that he will not forget but more importantly something that has set some very good foundations for his ability to learn in the future.

I hope that this project will continue further into Cameron's education and I also hope that even more children will be given the same opportunity, as this is a very valuable educational tool. (Tracy Fricker)

A parent's contribution to a seminar

I have always felt up to date with what my child has been doing at [Four Acres] school. I have lots of photographs and snippets of conversations that have taken place throughout his learning process. I consider myself so very fortunate to have so much background into the beginning of his learning journey. It has enabled us as a family to talk about the things he has experienced and go into more detail. It's a way of sharing and remembering the tiny details that unless they are logged or photographed, are memories gone forever, or memories I would never have had the opportunity to share. I would ask any parents with older children to think back and try to recall the funny things your child said or did. You may recall a few. But are you as fortunate as I have been – have you got the evidence?

I think every child and parent should be involved in this history making and feel sad for those who are not. My child thrived at [school] and without the documentation and learning diary to keep me informed, his learning would all have been a well kept, closely guarded secret. (Denise, parent of Aaron at Four Acres school, Bristol)

6
Artists in 5x5x5=creativity

This chapter considers the role of the artists who work in 5x5x5=creativity. They discuss their perceptions and resonances with a strong sense of shared experience and learning, of listening, responding to and developing children's fascinations within collaborative learning contexts. The exploration of creativity in children and adults, and the vibrant involvement of artists, is a vital part of our research. 5x5x5 has a community of artists working at the forefront of research.

Emily Pringle (2003) talks about 'artists in educational contexts' and how artists can provide positive teaching and learning experiences without compromising their own artistic practice or that of others. The open-ended, critically-reflective and collaborative forms of engagement the artists and participants enter into is not only fundamental to current ideas around creative teaching and learning but also – and perhaps more importantly – central to and inspired by the nature of creative practice itself. It is this link between creative practice and pedagogy that is crucial: the artists engage with participants primarily through discussion and exchanging ideas and experiences. There is evidence of 'co-constructive' learning taking place, whereby shared knowledge is generated.

The artist functions as co-learner, rather than as an infallible expert transmitting knowledge to the participants. Artists promote experiential learning, with an emphasis on giving participants the opportunity to experiment within a supportive environment. The relationship between the artists' individual creative practice and their collaborative or pedagogic work is, therefore, critical. When working with participants, the artists draw on their own education, training, and ongoing creative activities in order to engage and inspire

153

participants and enable them to explore their own ideas. It is a unique and sophisticated form of engagement.

a) The role of the artist in 5x5x5=creativity
Deborah Aguirre Jones and Gill Nicol
edited by Penny Hay and Mary Fawcett

5x5x5=creativity artists

Many different kinds of artists are employed within the project. They work in different media: music, dance, theatre, sound and visual art, each artist bringing an impressive range of expertise and knowledge. They have enquiring minds, are open to ideas and to change, have lateral thinking skills and are good collaborators and communicators. They must also have experience of working with young children. Many already have knowledge of different learning styles – audio, visual and kinaesthetic – as these are practices they use on a daily basis.

An artist working within the 5x5x5 programme challenges the existing tradition of the artists-in-schools model in the UK. The conventional and dominant model many educators already work, or have worked with, perceives the artist as an expert. Their role is to display a set of practical skills, in order to teach the children – hopefully as many as possible – a new way of making art. The result is an end product, either made by each individual – a pot for example – to take home, or one big piece in which every child's input is visible – eg a mosaic in the playground. In the last five years there has been a growing awareness of the importance of creative thinking within our teaching frameworks and the role artists can play. 'The practitioner must create a climate where curiosity is encouraged and where children can experience the unexpected' (QCA, 2000).

5x5x5 takes as its starting point the inspiring way of working in preschools in Reggio Emilia. Here the artist is known as the *atelierista* and their role is identified thus:

> The *atelierista* is a studio worker, an artisan, a lender of tools, a partner in a quest or journey. In this way you are a maker, but maybe more richly you are an enabler, someone who will attend to others in their creation, their development and their communication of knowledge. (Vecchi in Edwards *et al*, 1998)

In Reggio Emilia an *atelierista* will be someone who has a teaching qualification specialising in art, who enables and facilitates the children.

5x5x5 looks to extend that role by advertising for 'professional artists of out-standing calibre' (Fawcett and Hay, 2003), who are predominantly artists with an ongoing, professional, contemporary arts practice. 'The aim of these artists is to enable, facilitate, collaborate and co-research with people – both children and adults ...'

Reggio *atelieristas* will be appointed full time, as an integrated member of the staff team at a preschool. The artists working with 5x5x5, however, are con-tracted on a freelance basis for between 15 and 20 days across one year although the aspiration is to have longer term contracts. Already some chil-dren's centres are taking on artists on a salaried basis.

The model of the 5x5x5 artist differs from both the Reggio Emilia *atelierista* and the traditional artist-in-schools model in these ways:

- The 5x5x5 artist has an ongoing practice in the field of contemporary art, working with conceptual as well as material processes and operating within the broader sphere of cultural production. The *atelierista* is someone with a range of visual representational and practical skills but usually does not have their own artistic practice. The traditional artist-in-schools model does not require the artist to think conceptually or laterally within the delivery of their education practice.

- The 5x5x5 artist is working outside their own discipline, as a visitor to the educational profession which has different frames of ontological, epistemological and evaluative reference to those of the art world, whereas the *atelierista* is part of a team of educators continually working together and developing a shared language of research and dialogue.

- The 5x5x5 artist is a freelancer, without the security of a salaried post or other organisational supports of an employee, whereas an *atelierista* is a member of staff and has full-time employment and relative security.

- The 5x5x5 artist has the luxury of working over a period of a year, building relationships, unlike the traditional UK model of artists in schools, which usually entails one or two days of intensive activity focusing solely on practical issues.

The comparison between these three models reveals the experimental, risk-taking approach of 5x5x5. The role and position of the artist within 5x5x5 is still being invented and evolved, unlike the stable and well established role of the *atelierista* in Reggio preschools. It is not a question of seeking to identify one or the other as 'better' or 'worse', but rather of finding our own model within the context of UK culture and curriculum demands. We can identify differences that need to be acknowledged, engaged with, supported and celebrated. It is perhaps simplistic to compartmentalise these differences so clearly. For example, within 5x5x5, the artist can model a new medium, technique or way of thinking to offer a provocation or focus. This borrows from the traditional way of working but it is reframed to support and extend children's learning in an action/reflection cycle.

Key characteristics of 5x5x5 artists
Artist/provocateur

> I am looking for ways of opening up the creative process so it is possible to work alongside other artists to jointly create work, without a hierarchical structure of specific roles. (Kathy Hinde)

> This relates to my art practice through the problem solving mechanism such as playing with materials, putting together ideas formerly unrelated and allowing ideas to surface. I also try to go with an idea sometimes even though I have no idea where it will go, but be prepared to enjoy the journey. (Jenni Dutton)

> The focus is on fascination, not on attainment and outcomes. This is also how I like to approach my own work. It is reassuring to be in this environment. The time allocated for the importance of reflection will also help me do the same for myself. In reflecting on what has already been done, threads can appear which enable me to go deeper with future work. These would otherwise remain latent. The joy and inspiration I gain from working with children will inevitably feed into my own work. (Cathy Mills)

> There's a question for me, am I an authority (as artist) or an outsider? It's far less easy for me to behave as an outsider, a provocateur, who does nonsensical things and goes off on tangents – when I am also being a 'trainer' who reassures, someone who others see as an expert. The new staff look to me, as they know I have been involved a long time. (Deborah Jones)

Co-researcher with adults and children

> I perceive my role to be that of an artistic collaborator – to ... venture out on a wild, anarchic, creative voyage into the unknown, creating our map as we go. (Jo Harvey)

> We had these fantastic conversations where we really did bounce ideas off each other and it felt energetic and inspiring. What was great was that [the educator] allowed open-endedness. Allowed us to change our minds without letting other teaching obligations get in the way. (Kathy Hinde)

[I see myself as]

- a co-creator alongside the children, open and attentive to their ideas and interests and engaging with them in a playful way

- a collaborator with early years practitioners in the setting, with the intention of supporting the children's creativity

- a researcher, taking time to reflect on my experience of working creatively with children and to gain understandings and insights which will develop my practice and also feed into the larger picture of the 5x5x5 research project. (Annabelle McFayden)

We are researching ourselves researching children researching the world.
(Deborah Jones and Kirsty Claxton)

Increasingly, there are some artists who will not automatically locate the child as their area of research and inquiry. They are likely to be interested in re-searching the context of the research, ie extending the focus to also consider the 5x5x5 project, the adults working together, themselves, the educational context; indeed pedagogy itself.

It is possible from this wealth of evidence to identify key characteristics of arts practitioners who are working on 5x5x5 as:

- opening not closing

- aspiring to be non-hierarchical

- identifying a parallel approach between personal art practice and 5x5x5

- problem-solving through play

- engaging in emergent thinking

- risk-taking

- conducting process-led work

- provoking original thinking

- working with and valuing others

- building trust

- delving deeper

- constantly asking questions

- questioning own position – not fixed in a role

- acknowledging the dynamics of change

- responding with joy and passion

- co-creating knowledge

- working alongside, not in front

- having shared values and dialogue with educators

- recognising the importance of reflection and the time needed for it.

Why do the artists want to be involved?

The arts allow you to try out different versions of yourself. (Kirsty Claxton)

Because of its research emphasis, 5x5x5 gives integrity to the artists' research and their work. The emphasis is on process that is collaborative and participatory, which is close to many artists' methodology. And artists are drawn to the growing national reputation of the project.

The project is long-term, compared to most of the educational work offered to creative practitioners. The educators and artists get to know each other well and gain a deep understanding of the other's practice, offering the potential for lasting relationships where meaningful changes and significant learning can occur.

This work has the capacity to enrich the artist as a practitioner and this is an area we are exploring further. Artists are paid fairly and have the certainty of a contracted block of days spread out over a specified time; which gives freelancers much needed practical support.

Integrated professional development

The artists arrive with differing perceptions of 5x5x5, and the challenge is to provide appropriate support via initial training and continuing professional development. Such training is vital, because we cannot assume a shared ethic between the artist, educator and mentor. Training is an arena in which a strong relationship can develop between the key partners, educator and artist, and disabuse each of any stereotyped notions of the other.

It was important that we developed a mutual trust and respect, accepting the fact that we are all coming from different places (Carrie Beckett, educator)

5x5x5 speaks back to me – one of the joys of the research is the possibility of a moment when the project opens up and something is revealed to me as part of my own practice. (Deborah Jones)

It has helped me to think more and paint less, to stand back and think about how I am approaching my work, think about the world I am entering. (Kay Lewis Bell)

Working on the project gives artists the confidence to explore 'letting go' within other spheres of their practice:

Uncovering the importance of listening to children and following their ideas has changed my approach to the way I work outside the project ... more freedom and less structure ... not that I did not have it before, but 5x5x5 allowed me to feel what it's like. As a creator myself, the work with children has provoked the production of a piece of theatre to use with other children. (Annabelle Macfadyen)

Doing the project, coming to seminars, having conversations with others and the mentor – it feels like I'm thinking more about the processes of creativity in relation to other work I do. (Kathy Hinde)

The art of looking

It's such a big feature of 5x5x5 – 'looking and being looked at'. The artist's familiarity with processes of documentation is key. The artist brings fresh eyes to the setting so will notice the subtle and significant things that happen there. Their ability to observe, and the ongoing investigation with representation enable them to communicate what is visible in different ways.

Sometimes watching the children was almost like me – watching me or me watching my theatre company. (Michael Loader)

It's hard being watched and documented when you don't know where it is going. By the end I felt more confident to direct in the moment – to play around more with this way of working, of how I frame ideas with them. (Rachel Sinclair)

Ways forward

As 5x5x5 grows and more artists come on board, questions are being raised around the potential for development as artists within the project. For instance, should artists make art within the project?

It has become evident that artists need to come together more often to share and learn from each other.

More contact with other artists in a no-agenda meeting would be good. I've learnt a lot of theory of education, but actually the thing of talking with other artists is how those get translated into art-making practice. The other thing is that because artists aren't embedded in research language, things get articulated in different ways. (Kathy Hinde)

There is scope for a celebration and acknowledgement of the range of different practices that artists bring.

In terms of skill I'd like the opportunity to feed in new skills as the need arises. I feel the need for the opportunity to increase my own skill base, ie computer or animation skills. At the moment there have not been any opportunities for the artists to develop their own skills by accessing the expertise of other artists in 5x5x5. (Tessa Richardson Jones)

Questions

Many questions continue to be asked within the project. This reflects the in-depth enquiry and research that goes on between all the participants. There can, however, be a tension around the process of ongoing questioning, alongside the output-orientated requirements of the curriculum. Some of the questions being asked by artists are vital for exploring a dialogue of discovery for themselves and others:

- How does 5x5x5 fit into an artist's practice – what space and time does it take up?

- How do we manage the growing expectations of being involved in 5x5x5 as its reputation continues to grow?

- Do the artists become children?

- What dialogue happens between the work with the children and the artists' practice elsewhere?

- What are the implications of the difference between the children performing and the processes of documentation (silent and separate documenter, digital camera, video camera, note book and pen) compared to an adult who is working creatively with them?

- What is the difference between the child as researcher and the child as artist or performer?

- Does this project speak to the art world?

- How much could or should the educator and setting know about the artist and their world?

b) AND (Artists Network Development)

Penny Hay, Catherine Lamont Robinson and Karen Wallis

5x5x5 has been described predominantly in educational language to date. In 2006 the 5x5x5 team consulted a group of experienced 5x5x5 artists and this led to a text defining the development in an artists' research group: AND. Funding from Arts Council England South West in 2007 has enabled the research to engage more in artists' professional development in the context of the arts world.

AND is a 5x5x5 artist-led initiative that has developed in response to our artists' request for time to work together to analyse the impact of 5x5x5 not only on the children but their own practice as artists. This is an under-researched subject nationally and the lessons learned will be of interest to the wider sector. AND also aims to broaden and deepen the opportunities for professional development for artists working with 5x5x5. Built into the artists' contracts is time for reflection and discussion. This gives us the opportunity to research the role of the artist in some depth and this additional programme, designed by the artists, will enable them to explore how 5x5x5 works and what its effect on their own practice is and could be when:

- working with others – the challenges and opportunities

- working with children and adults from different cultural backgrounds.

They can also examine experience elsewhere in the UK and abroad, examine how 5x5x5=creativity affects our other practice as artists, and refine the language used to describe what is happening.

AND was set in motion with an artists' blog and artist-led sessions as part of the whole research group's professional development. Accreditation for artists and their research with 5x5x5 is currently being investigated.

The background to AND

The position of 5x5x5 is unique. 5x5x5 artists differ from the usual UK model of artists-in-schools as visiting experts and from the *atelieristas* (see page 154) of Reggio Emilia. 5x5x5 artists are freelance practitioners from many disciplines who come into the educational setting wearing their artist's hat, to act as provocateurs in 5x5x5 research.

The 5x5x5 artists are working outside their usual familiar environment and the first steps are to perform a subtle dance with the educators as we each recognise the other's perspectives about the research and how it will impact on the children and school. This stage is not yet as visible as the hands-on research but it is arguably of equal importance. Only by sensitively building relationships with the staff and children can the research ethos of 5x5x5 take root.

5x5x5 artists need to be recognised for their difference and their value in the overall 5x5x5 research programme. They have to have a voice, with which to contribute to the 5x5x5 research programme. The artists should have development opportunities as artists in their own right within the 5x5x5 experience and connect it with their own practice.

Many artists have said they want space and time to talk informally as a group to help sustain their practice and stimulate new lines of enquiry about the diverse range of interests and experience within the artist group and the values we share. At an artists' picnic, for example, artists had the chance to pool their diverse range of interests and experience.

> AND gives me the opportunity to develop my own interests in how we interact with the world. I was able to use the AND picnic to explore the way we as artists connect 5x5x5 with our own practice and to learn about all our different approaches to research. (Karen Wallis)

The fluid, boundary-pushing, unpredictable aspect of 5x5x5 is something in which children excel, yet adults often let the opportunity slip through their fingers. Catherine sums up what she feels and what AND sets out to preserve when she says:

> To be playful is not to be trivial or frivolous, or to act as though nothing of consequence will happen. On the contrary, when we are playful with each other we relate as free persons, and the relationship is open to surprise, everything that happens is of consequence. (Carse, 1987)

Professional development

In professional development sessions integrated throughout the research the artists give presentations of their work. Ongoing sharing of reflections and documentation are a key part of the learning for all the adults involved. The artist-educator-cultural centre partnership underpins the authenticity of the research. Artists can bring new insights and a sense of the 'other' to these relationships through creative exploration of this kind. The annual exhibitions are strongly influenced by an aesthetic of art education and discussion is underway to share and curate them in a mutually accessible way. A 5x5x5 artists' forum can be a resource for ideas, a conversation or a 'library' for research.

I'm in different places at once, partly integrated and partly not, partly separate. My practice is my art as well as my sensibilities, and my art struggles to find a place ... Research is moving through change. Being changed. Inventing and finding meanings, with other people and through the languages we invent together. (Deborah Jones)

AND's future

The practices of 5x5x5 artists are all highly individual. The artists contribute in their unique way to 5x5x5 and also to the development of AND. AND can express the power that artists bring to 5x5x5. Each year there will be a new AND group, with a few artists from previous years for continuity, who will be able to make things happen for children and artists.

c) An artist's journal
Catherine Lamont-Robinson
edited by Susi Bancroft and Mary Fawcett

Catherine was the 5x5x5 artist at St Mary's Infant School, Marlborough, Wiltshire during 2005-6. She, like other artists and educators, kept a personal journal of her 5x5x5 experiences.

I have found that art and education have always gone hand in hand. Having completed a BA and Masters in Fine Art followed by PGCE (Postgraduate Certificate in Education), I began working in Further and Higher Education as an art tutor whilst continuing my own practice – painting and drawing.

I had always been fascinated by the psychological/neurological aspects of visual perception and when my daughter Shannon started school I began a Doctorate of Education investigating how art practice can support visually impaired children. My own studio work underwent a radical and welcome shift as I worked increasingly with clay and mixed media.

My research draws upon autobiographical material and current neurological findings and my chosen methodology is longitudinal case studies. Once my doctorate was completed I was keen to ground my academic research and 5x5x5= creativity provided the perfect opportunity.

The ethos, observational and analytical aspects of this research are close to my heart. My time with the children at St. Mary's has not only reinforced a passionate belief in the educational potential of the cognitive and creative process but has also revitalised and extended my perspective as an artist.

At St Mary's school the adults involved were Rebecca, a reception class teacher, Mary, a teaching assistant and documenter, Rosemary, the 5x5x5 mentor and Sandra, the headteacher.

The action took place in the Spring Term. Some activities involved the whole reception class of children aged 4 and 5, on other occasions Catherine worked with smaller groups.

An extract from Catherine's journal follows.

Provocation for following session

The children have been asked to bring in outdoor gear for a walk to the local forest. It will be interesting to see if the recurring references dens and vertical structures will resurface during the visit. We shall bring along magnifying glasses, string, scissors, tape and balls of clay ...

Session 4 – *The full year-group, both reception teachers, Rebecca and Alison, Mary and myself.*

Description

The walk

I began the session with a visualisation exercise before the walk: I asked the children to close their eyes while I took them through an imaginary multi-sensory journey. This included a dramatic location and climate changes such as walking through a field of freshly fallen snow, pushing their toes into wet and dry sand, lying on their backs in a warm sea – what did their fingers touch below the surface? – listening to noises in a wood, feeling the rain on their faces and so on ... The purpose was to encourage the children to be aware of a variety of sensory input emphasising weight, movement, distance and quality of light in addition to information from the five senses.

We then set off taking the materials mentioned and several empty carrier bags for our finds. Some of the spontaneous observations included reference to the movement of the ivy up the tree-trunks and along the branches, the dusting of frost on the ground, grass sprouting out of unexpected places, the length and shapes of roots and how they 'keep the tree straight', what might live under the roots at the base of trees – mice were suggested – tracks in the mud underfoot. Two trees with overlapping branches which we walked underneath were dubbed 'umbrella-trees'; others mentioned 'fairy trees' and tree spirits and one child pointed out a 'spider-tree' indicating its intricate web of low branches.

When we stopped at a picnic bench in the clearing to have a snack I asked the group what had caught their interest. Jessica mentioned the pattern we made meandering through the trees. The notion that during the walk we had 'the whole forest to ourselves' was also raised. There was minimal reference to sounds in the environment but when encouraged to listen hard the children isolated sounds such as the birds moving in the trees above and the drip of melting frost falling onto the leaves below. When we split up into two groups again and the children were asked to select something to observe closely, their attention became more focused. Toby pointed out that one upright branch formation looked like a 'walrus's tooth', several children became very interested in different types of fungi and moss, some chose trees for the roughness of their barks, others for the pale, smooth, peeling textures. A large frozen puddle caused the boys great excitement and, unsurprisingly, the block of muddy ice was levered away and smashed into smaller fragments. Several leaves, pieces of twig and bark, were collected by the children and one of the smallest girls, Serena, insisted on carrying back a large log which looked almost half her size. She managed to inveigle a team of us into carrying it in turns after a brave initial stretch.

The classroom session

The session started with a brief look at the array of collected objects and many of the children's observations related to the variety of colours, textures, patterns and forms.

I suggested that the group make a painting to reflect their morning. Paint was provided and the children spent time selecting appropriate brushes.

Ethan immediately selected a toothbrush and started a painting of his muddy shoe. He took a piece of black paper and became intensely absorbed, covering small areas at a time in patches of subtle blues, greens, greys and purples.

Three of the girls started painting a large, centrally-placed image of the classic stereotypical child's tree – mid-brown trunk adorned with a bright green cloud of foliage. However, they then started to modify their initial images. Talia had selected black, and painted white around the tree to depict frost, Amy mixed browns and greens for the mud, started to add branches to the tree and later darkened the image in various parts with black paint, and carefully added a subtle range of pale greens. Her sky was white with a touch of grey-green.

Jessica had initially combined brown and green on the trunk and went on to paint red roots. She announced 'I'm doing a tree. Some people think trees are green at the top and brown at the bottom – but I've seen red!' Jessica kept changing the size of her brush according to her needs, using a small brush to make patterns on the trunk and asking for the toothbrush to indicate the grass. She also added black to the tree, mentioning that it had been dark in the forest, and finally included people walking through the forest into her painting. Jessica's final touches to the trunk were circular blobs which she referred to as 'the lumpy bits on the tree'.

Serena painted directly onto the log we had lugged back from the forest very carefully and with intense concentration, mixing a rainbow of exotic Gauguin-like colours, giving a running commentary on the mixing, and singing as she proceeded. She carefully attached a leaf to the surface and mentioned some seeds embedded in the bark at intervals.

Reflection

I was surprised when the three girls reverted to the classic representation of a generalised tree as a starting point, yet all had modified their imagery from observations on the walk as the paintings developed – although a few memory-triggering hints were dropped. It seemed that intense involvement with the materials, in particular the colour-mixing, stimulated their memory and enriched their responses. The group had only received one colour-mixing session from Mary previously yet I have never before seen such awareness of colour nuances in a group of 4 and 5 year olds. Noting my delight, they were very keen to verbalise their particular choices of colours and explain how they were matching the shade of the cloudy sky, muddy frost, etc. All of the children were highly absorbed in this session. Indeed Serena went into a world of her own as the log became a vibrant palette.

The children seem to be demonstrating confidence to tackle a wide array of materials, it would be interesting to give the next group materials other than paint to start with and see if the tendency to return to previous stylisations still emerges. Rebecca, Mary and I had a fruitful discussion about the role of the artist as regards intervention and provocation and they requested that I lead the next session in my role as artist with a demonstration if appropriate.

Provocation for the following session

I shall bring in a small selection of my own work based on observations from nature, in particular trees, leaves, nests, etc, using a variety of materials including paint, collage, a clay relief and some close-up photographs. After the introduction the children will observe some nearby trees and select those they wish to create an image from, take a clay print of the bark, a rubbing, and memorise the colours, textures forms and so on to create a collage of their observations.

After the project

I asked James and Jessica what they thought 'the project was about' and how they felt about the sessions.

James started off: 'It was fun and like being a real artist – like you.'

Jessica: 'I think that the trees that we made were like real trees, I was looking very carefully!'

James added: 'It's given me flies in my brain – it changes the way I think and I make with my hands.' I asked him to give me an example and he replied: 'looking at the materials first and then my brain gives me ideas ... tearing and twisting things ...'

Jessica concluded: 'Now you've got me into making real art and I enjoy making things at home.'

7

Cultural centres and 5x5x5=creativity

Kate Cross and Penny Hay

What is a cultural setting in 5x5x5?

Over the past seven years, 5x5x5=creativity has worked with a wide variety of cultural centres. The initiative began in 2000, linking schools with contemporary art practice and educators working with galleries and artists. The galleries were the first funders of the project in its pilot phase. We have since extended our focus to include cultural centres such as museums, theatres, arts and outdoor learning organisations. Members of the cultural staff teams are seen as researchers in companionship with children. As in Reggio Emilia, the cultural community take charge of the learning alongside teams of artists and educators.

In the UK, cultural centres large and small applauded the publication of Ken Robinson's *All Our Futures* (NACCCE, 1999) and believed it to be a timely critique on the British education system. It lent gravitas to their own education initiatives, challenged their thinking and gave rise to public cries from such flagship institutions as The Royal National Theatre, The Southbank Centre and Tate Modern for cultural-based learning in schools.

Cultural centres often have a learning culture at the heart of their mission. Centres are invited to join the research as a reciprocal arrangement to inform the learning culture of their organisation. Through the research they are developing a deepening dialogue with educators and partnerships with schools to 'make learning vivid and real' (*National Primary Strategy*, 2004). The recent government commitment to five hours of culture a week in

167

schools raises many questions about how this should be integrated into educational and arts provision. We need to move away from time-limited initiatives into life-long systemic change. Robinson argued in 1999: 'a national strategy for creative and cultural education is essential'.

One of our aims was to support the partnerships with a wide range of cultural organisations, to respond to the developing ideas of children. The engagement of the centres has largely come about as a result of an invitation to be involved with the research. Sometimes the link is a natural development providing the context for the art form focus. For example in a nursery where the line of enquiry was focusing on non-verbal communication, the drama and movement practitioner works in partnership with a local theatre. Others links are identified in direct response to the children's interests and their lines of enquiry. Some are places in the locality with no education team attached (such as woodlands). Where it works well 'an enriched relationship benefits the whole school', such as Moorlands Infant School, Bath working with the Holburne Museum.

Staff from the cultural centres may host venue based sessions or visit schools, engaging with children alongside artists and educators. By extending the learning environment and space in which they work, the cultural centres can develop long-term relationships with settings. Often the cultural partner will act as a mentor for the artist. We also strive to develop a shared-language about learning and research across the cultural, arts and education sectors. The involvement of parents is also key, often bringing in new audiences in harder to reach areas. In many galleries and art museums, parents have seen children taking responsibility for exhibiting their own work. Many venue based centres offer opportunities for parents to share in the learning process.

> ... 5x5x5 has helped us to develop a more in depth understanding and relationship with our partner schools, thus strengthening our understanding of schools' practice and of children's learning, growing and creativity therein. In turn this informs delivery across other areas of our remit. (Kate Cross and Nick White, the egg theatre for children and young people, Bath)

Working with such an open-ended approach can present challenges for cultural centres, as the nature of their programmes often defines a focus in advance. There may be tension between the idea of being flexible so as to fit with emergent work, and still operating a core programme. Time is required to develop work in settings in partnership with colleagues outside it. The notion of partnership is attractive but achieving it requires careful attention to building mutual confidence and trust between the various practitioners.

Addressing preconceptions about the purposes of cultural centres can generate useful dialogue. The challenges of logistics and resources can be crucial. Many cultural centres would prefer to offer their expertise or venue as an alternative site for learning, so that the extraordinary visit becomes an ordinary part of a learning culture. 5x5x5 places value on children's access to different creative environments for learning with adults other than their teachers.

The egg theatre in Bath, for example, welcomes the opportunity to develop a long lasting relationship with a specific group of children by regularly hosting their research on site. Their very presence would permeate the organisation and provoke meaningful dialogue with other groups the theatre works with. In practice, however, this can pose logistical issues that are sometimes difficult for the school to overcome.

Time must be allocated for cultural centres to be involved more fully in the research. The aim is to provide a funding cycle that will achieve stability and nurture long-term relationships. It is also possible to formalise relationships across cultural centres so that children have the chance to see other work going on. Sound planning, adequate resourcing and ongoing commitment are essential for such effective partnerships to grow.

The impact of 5x5x5 on the partner organisation

Many of our partner organisations have developed their learning culture in tandem with our work. The philosophical impetus for the egg theatre, for instance, has been developed out of a shared commitment to supporting and developing children's ideas. The egg at Theatre Royal Bath was conceived and designed in association with young people. There is a strong reciprocal relationship between the staff at the egg and the 5x5x5 research team.

Organisations such as Swainswick Explorers are eager for the children to lead with their ideas and encounter less adult intervention. They take fewer resources out with them and instead are inspired by the children's self-initiated learning. Black Swan Arts have reduced their planned activity and respond instead to children's ideas as a result of the project.

> It has been good to be involved with a high profile research project, deepen our relationship with the teacher, school and artists involved. (Louise, Black Swan Arts)

Salisbury Arts Centre has been involved with 5x5x5=creativity for two years and the philosophy of 5x5x5 is now at its core and beginning to permeate the whole organisation. The emphasis has been on following ideas rather than

Edwina Bridgeman's exhibition of Paradise at the Victoria Art gallery, Bath.

outcome, creating a sense of greater openness. The Merlin Theatre identified how 5x5x5 ideas have informed the artists' work – this in turn led to more workshops at the theatre, with allied benefits. The profile of the project has often helped centres to obtain more funding.

Cultural centres had a role as both provider and beneficiary. The project's high profile has attracted positive attention and new networks. In local, regional and national press, 5x5x5 speaks to education but less to the arts and cultural press.

5x5x5=creativity has a strong philosophy of working to develop long term research and evaluation in partnership.

> Change is a constant process, not an event. Organisations themselves need to be reflexive and to learn. They need constantly to revisit and reaffirm their values. According to MIT Professor Peter Senge, the most vibrant, resilient, successful and profitable organisations display a set of learning behaviours. These are to:

- think and enquire
- challenge assumptions and stimulate debate
- collaborate and discuss
- create feedback loops
- develop a common language, and
- create a shared understanding and taxonomy.

These behaviours need to be continuous and embedded. (Holden, 2008, *Learning Culture*: Consultation Paper for the Clore Duffield Foundation)

Cultural centres working with 5x5x5 have found new ways of engaging children and adults in their learning. Together we have explored the value of an open-ended and heuristic approach, negotiating the complexities and challenges involved. Adults have experienced changing roles, becoming a collaborator, learner, researcher, creative enabler, listener, observer, documenter, mentor, artist, curator, critic. By using documentation to build a body of convincing work 5x5x5 provides evidence which can be used to challenge existing frameworks. Its support of professional learning networks and its work with families and communities offers the potential for transforming practice. 5x5x5 creates a space for creative reflective practice where relationships are central to making change.

8

5x5x5=creativity:
our learning, our legacy

Penny Hay

Our learning journey over the past decade has been full of amazing moments, beyond any expectations. 5x5x5 has been an open-ended adventure, maintaining great respect for the infinite capacity of children's imagination and creativity. The research team regularly revisits and reviews recurring themes and questions, theories and fascinations so as to understand learning more profoundly and offer new possibilities to others.

Democratic and creative learning communities
Access, democracy and participation are the key principles that have underpinned our collaborative work. The willingness and open minds of the adults we work with have allowed us to take purposeful risks together. Uncertainty and mutual trust coexist comfortably.

> ... to recognise doubt and uncertainty, to recognise your limits as a resource, as a place of encounter, as a quality. Which means that you accept that you are unfinished, in a state of permanent change, and your identity is in the dialogue. (Rinaldi, 2006)

Creative and reflective learning communities have been developed for teachers as well as children, parents and others who are interested in being involved. The research values the processes of reflection, experimentation, documentation and responsive planning. Time and space are allocated to develop a conversational approach to learning together. The project has created a virtual, reflective space that nurtures professional growth and debate: a democratic and creative research community.

Some useful implications for learning and pedagogy have emerged. The adult's role is co-participative and inclusive; discourse and the co-construction of knowledge are vital. Adults and children work together in a climate of creative enquiry to seek new connections.

A willingness to observe, listen and work closely with children's ideas has developed in a community of adults who understand what it means to be creative, who are interested in how children learn and who model the creative process alongside children.

> Creativity should not be considered a separate mental faculty, but a characteristic of our way of thinking, knowing and making choices. (Edwards *et al*, 1998)

The child at the heart of the process

Children will always come up with good ideas, with unexpected theories that are purposeful and imaginative. Careful observations of children provide insight into their interests and pre-occupations. The adults facilitate and support the children's depth of learning by respecting their individual interests and taking time to make connections with the children's thinking. The emphasis is on supporting children's developing ideas, thoughts and feelings. The children are given opportunities for exploration, for response and contextualisation of their learning, using innovative and imaginative approaches that stimulate the imagination and encourage independent thought.

If adults take children's ideas seriously they can support children in the exploration and expression of their ideas in a 'hundred languages'. Documentation to 'make the learning visible' is integral to the process.

The invisible framework

Participants are partners in critical enquiry. The project offers a clear framework without prescription for the enquiries. The 'invisible framework' (see chapter 3) supports the integrated professional development, peer mentoring support and the supportive networks which are being created at different levels so that individuals, schools, artists, parents and cultural centres share and discuss practice.

The significance of the arts

The effect of this collegiate research has opened new horizons in relation to multi-disciplinary discourse and has highlighted the importance of self-reflection. Multi-sensory and multi-modal learning approaches (see chapter 4) have developed the notion of learning as a multi-dimensional concept. The arts raise the human condition and enrich personal experience, they give us

174

a sense of identity, stretch our intellectual and emotional responses and help us become more flexible and creative in our attitudes (Steers and Swift, 1999).

The arts have the power to be transformational in our lives and this is affirmed by the work of 5x5x5. The arts are an important element of our lives. Working alongside creative professional artists has been a privilege that all children and adults should have access to: to be able to learn together in ways that value our human capacities for being creative, for being artists.

The research has recorded the exploration of big themes: identity, belonging, community, relationships, conflict, birth and death. Giving attention to different interpretations and fluid meanings in constructing knowledge has generated 'possibility thinking with wisdom': creative thinking and social responsibility (Craft, 2005).

> Otto (4) was talking to me about being an artist, it is obviously something which he is passionate about, he asked if he could be my helper at the exhibition when he was grown up or maybe even a teenager. I said 'of course and that I would look forward to it', he went away and came back a bit later to ask if I would still be alive when he was grown up, a very important consideration! (Edwina, artist)

Adults learning together

As researchers we are constantly exploring new ways of learning. Valuing curiosity, ingenuity, playfulness, imagination and risk enables adults to immerse themselves in complex ideas, reflect on them and distil their essence for their own and others' learning. Artists and cultural settings working in the context of education have helped to develop a creative ethos with the support of an experienced team of mentors. 5x5x5=creativity has built a critical mass of creative reflective practitioners who have developed research as a habit of mind. Relationships built on trust, respect and responsibility are overarching features of the success of any partnership.

Transforming learning capacity

5x5x5 set out to make a difference: 'to transform learning capacity' (Drummond in Adams *et al*, 2004). The life chances of children can be improved through developing their confidence in themselves as creative learners, thinkers and problem solvers so that they become more motivated and engaged in their learning. Supporting a 'learning to learn' agenda will help equip children with the skills to view learning as a purposeful pursuit and become independent, lifelong learners.

Siraj-Blatchford *et al* (2002) advocate an environment of enquiry and a culture of 'sustained shared thinking' – open-ended conversations that are genuinely child-led, with adults scaffolding thinking by getting involved in the thinking process themselves. Adults can't learn for the children; they have to learn for themselves. We need to see children as powerful learners who learn from each other and learn together. Sustained shared thinking builds on children's interests and understandings, making connections in learning in a shared enquiry where adults and children together question, debate, hypothesise and reflect on their ideas together.

Creative and critical thinking

Creativity and creative thinking are at the heart of this *EYFS* agenda as they provide the bridge between the cognitive and affective domains of learning. When young children are encouraged to think creatively by following their own lines of enquiry, establishing hypotheses about the world, exploring possibilities, making new connections and solving problems, they are developing the skills of life long learning. When their ideas and feelings are sought and valued and they are encouraged to decide for themselves how they can best represent these ideas, through story making, painting, sculpture, dance, role play or music for example, they come to see themselves as citizens of the world who can make a positive contribution to their community. In this way they develop strong dispositions to learning and confidence in themselves, both as people and as learners. (Sally, Jaeckle, Director for the Foundation Stage, DCSF and 5x5x5=creativity Trustee)

5x5x5=creativity is creating an environment where thinking processes are transparent, valued and shared, where adults are willing to observe, listen and work closely with children's ideas with endless curiosity. Studies by Cremin *et al* (2006) confirm the strategies which support possibility thinking as being 'standing back', 'profiling learner agency' and 'creating time and space'.

What counts is the maturity of the adults who accompany the children. The priority of these adults is not 'moulding' children. Instead their aim is to strengthen children's capacities – which can only happen through the active involvement of children themselves. (Cremin *et al*, 2006)

Well-being and self esteem

The way 5x5x5 works supports the emotional well-being and self-esteem of both children and adults. It enhances individual creativity and the possibilities for personalised learning and reflects the learning styles, interests, preferences and needs of the learner. It follows their individual learning journeys to support progression, instill confidence and encourage positive dispositions to learning.

We have developed a culture of openness and enthusiasm, bringing together enquiring minds and a genuine desire to assist the children in their investigations.

Children's choice is at the heart of all the work we do as it informs a way forward and provides both children and adults with an open forum for discussion and debate. Without choice we would not be creating a culture of enquiry with opportunities for individual contributions and questions.

We have noticed the children leading and facilitating other children's ideas. The children are highly imaginative and eager to embrace a collective idea. Their language skills and ability to focus and concentrate for extremely long periods of time have been astounding. The children show their playfulness and desire for invention as they bounce ideas to and fro amongst the group. They have true respect for each others'* thoughts and ideas as they engage in discussion. At no time did we observe any disrespect. Their listening skills were exemplary and their thought processes both complex and philosophical. (Artists and educators in discussion at Freshford Primary School, Bath, 2007)

Notions about what constitutes a 'rich and stimulating environment' have become much more sophisticated. Some of the richest learning has taken place with very modest resources.

Paying genuine attention and being open to new possibilities – knowing that this may be difficult but embracing it anyway. Having huge optimism and a real capacity for joy and wonderment. Knowing that change is necessary for healthy growth and that it is truly better to light a candle than to curse the darkness ... it makes me constantly review my practice. (Gail, educator, Little Waves Children's Centre, North Somerset)

The evaluation report on 5x5x5 for Wiltshire local authority observed:

All of the educators and artists interviewed for this report concluded that it had changed their understanding and influenced their practice. For all the educators the experience had been transformational, enabling them to explore and introduce innovative practices, to reflect upon and discuss with others both the broad philosophy and the practical detail. (White, 2007)

A creative reflective pedagogy
In line with the *Every Child Matters* agenda, 5x5x5 supports children's holistic development through learning experiences that foster both cognitive and affective aspects of learning. The goal is to develop active citizens with rights, while offering an entitlement to a creative education. Adults need the courage to give children permission to be creative, to give more attention to the emotional, aesthetic and intellectual dimensions of learning.

When teachers can bring the curriculum alive by making learning meaningful and relevant to children, we have seen confident, aspirational learners result. (Sally Jaeckle, Director for the Foundation Stage, DCSF and 5x5x5=creativity Trustee)

177

Challenges and opportunities

There have been many challenges along the way: lack of funding, embedded views, reluctant participants, inadequate space, insecurities, lack of confidence, pressures of time, inconsistencies of support and personal tragedies. However, the longevity of the project has allowed relationships, dialogues, enquiries and reflections to deepen and evolve. Continuity and experience with the cycles of research foster confidence and rich evidence about creative learning has been generated.

The opportunities created by 5x5x5 have far outweighed the challenges. It has created time to reflect for a community of adults who are committed to supporting creative education. Various theoretical models have ensured that the research is intellectually rigorous.

Increasing numbers create new challenges: the integrity of the research process relies on the depth and quality of transformative dialogues. Liz, a mentor, describes her role as a 'positive place of encounter, of dialogue and research, where our role is to support the exploration of crisis and uncertainty, through our skills in orientation, meaning-making and values.'

Within 5x5x5's growing learning community, there is room to appreciate idiosyncratic practice and diverse lines of enquiry in pursuit of creative values, dispositions, environments and relationships. The recognition and respect for difference across the research groups has ensured a connectedness and collegiality in a supportive research environment among the cultural settings, their staff, mentors, artists, the children and their families. Through researching ourselves researching children researching the world, 5x5x5 is deepening our understanding of creativity. And through its reflective practice it is ensuring that the quality of every child's experience is strengthened and enhanced.

Now that 5x5x5 is a charitable company with a skilled and knowledgeable Board of Trustees, it is possible to plan for the long term. Success depends in large part on the quality of the artists, mentors and educators. The professional development is paying dividends in terms of the dissemination of findings, as the adults who experience the work first hand analyse and articulate what is happening. As a result they become ambassadors for the work in a wide variety of professional situations.

The loyalty of the adults involved in 5x5x5 indicates its track record. It has built up a core team of artists, experienced in the 5x5x5 approach. Educators frequently want to continue with the research for more than one year. We aim to balance this demand with the importance of moving on and involving new

178

settings. Many of the educators who have worked in the project have used their experience as the basis for studying further at Bath Spa University.

Most of the research is currently located in the Early Years Foundation Stage (0-6) and Key Stage 1 (5-7), although we are interested in the impact on whole settings and research with older children. We want to support local authorities in raising the quality of provision for all children, to improve their outcomes particularly in Communication, Language and Literacy and Personal, Social and Emotional Development, and to narrow the gap in achievement between the most and least advantaged. We want to reach policy makers, parents and carers, teachers, teaching assistants, artists, cultural centres and others involved in the education and development of children.

5x5x5 has elicited immense commitment and has enhanced confidence and mutual respect. The project has established a strong research ethic and a rigorous intellectual and emotional integrity that we hope will inform future policy.

Conclusions

> Our experience confirms that children need a great deal of freedom. the freedom to investigate and to try, to make mistakes and to correct mistakes, to choose where and with whom to invest their curiosity, intelligence and their emotions.

> Model on the adult level the kinds of democratic participation, collaborative learning, and conflict resolution you are trying to teach to the children. Negotiate not only such things as the choice of activities, but more fundamentally, negotiate the meaning. (Malaguzzi, 1993)

The priorities of 5x5x5 may be helpful in identifying what the purpose and values of education should be. Certain principles and approaches have proved effective, and they are listed here.

1. Learning how to learn should be central to any creative education initiative. The key learning dispositions to develop are: curiosity, imagination, creativity, independent thought, experimentation, negotiation, confidence, risk-taking, personal enquiry, self-confidence, self-esteem, enthusiasm, engagement and powerful thinking. Qualities such as empathy, playfulness, individuality, sensitivity, flexibility, problem solving and self-aware learning have to be nurtured.

2. The cognitive and the affective domains are equally important: the *Every Child Matters* agenda highlights both well-being and achievement. A recent UNICEF report states that British children are the un-

happiest in the developed world. Streaming, competition and punishment should be strongly opposed.

3. We need to support children's rights to a creative and democratic education and accept our responsibility as citizens with a clear sense of democracy, humanity, respect and tolerance.

4. Professionals such as teachers and artists offer wide expertise and support children's learning, but it should never be forgotten that parents are children's first educators.

5. Positive and creative relationships between adults and children are vital to nurture the disposition to learn and to engage them in meaningful learning experiences in which children take responsibility for their own learning.

6. Learning centres should be communities of reflection, enquiry and debate where research is a 'habit of mind' (Moss, 2003). Learning is deepened by developing metacognitive and self-reflective processes.

7. A dynamic, creative learning environment involves valuing different perspectives and different disciplines while maintaining a shared focus.

8. Freedom is possible within a structure: emphasis needs to be on a negotiated curriculum whereby children are given freedom within a structure to find independent ways of learning.

9. Creative values and supportive relationships help children develop a sense of belonging and personal identity.

10. The aim should be to develop a culture based on love, wonder, humility and compassion with endless intellectual curiosity, creativity and transformation (Kofman and Senge, 2001).

If we want to encourage a positive and responsible attitude in learners towards the complexities of choice, opportunities and obstacles facing us in the 21st Century, we cannot afford not to foster possibility thinking with wisdom in our classrooms. (Craft in Fisher, 2007).

5x5x5=creativity is a visionary, ground-breaking project which demonstrates the depth of learning fostered through exquisitely sensitive creative partnership. Children and adults involved in 5x5x5 are sowing seeds of systemic change in our education system, well beyond early years and primary, into secondary, further and higher education phases. (Tamsyn Imison, education strategist, and 5x5x5=creativity Trustee)

The research process of 5x5x5 is designed to deepen thinking, challenge perception and stimulate change. 5x5x5 is exploring exciting ways in which the creative and cultural community can be involved in meaningful learning with young children and their families. The investment in the creative talent of individuals can contribute to an educational culture that can change lives. The hope is to ensure that children and young people who have been involved with 5x5x5=creativity will be confident and creative thinkers in the future and succeed in all aspects of their lives.

No way. The hundred is there.

The child
is made of one hundred.
The child has
a hundred languages
a hundred hands
a hundred thoughts
a hundred ways of thinking
of playing, of speaking
A hundred always a hundred
ways of listening
of marvelling of loving
a hundred joys
for singing and understanding
a hundred worlds
to discover
a hundred worlds
to invent
a hundred worlds
to dream.
The child has
a hundred languages
(and a hundred hundred hundred more)
but they steal ninety-nine.
The school and the culture
separate the head from the body.
They tell the child:
to think without hands
to do without head
to listen and not to speak
to understand without joy
to love and to marvel
only at Easter and Christmas.
They tell the child:
to discover the world already there
and of the hundred
they steal ninety-nine.

They tell the child:
that work and play
reality and fantasy
science and imagination
sky and earth
reason and dream
are things
that do not belong together.

And thus they tell the child
that the hundred is not there.
The child says:
No way. The hundred is there.

Loris Malaguzzi

Translated by Lella Gandini, from *The Hundred Languages of Children Exhibition Catalogue* (Second edition, 1997). Published by Reggio Children. Copyright Preschools and Infant-toddler Centres – Istituzione of the Municipality of Reggio Emilia, Italy.

References

5x5x5=creativity 100 Voices. DVD from 5x5x5=creativity

Adams, S, Alexander, E, Drummond, MJ, and Moyles, J (2004) *Inside the Foundation Stage: Recreating the Reception Year.* London: Association of Teachers and Lecturers

Anning, A and Ring, K (2004) *Making Sense of Children's Drawings.* Maidenhead: Open University Press

Athey, C (1990) *Extending Thought in Young Children. A Parent-Teacher Partnership.* London: Paul Chapman Publishing

Austin, R (2007) *Letting the outside in: developing teaching and learning beyond the early years classroom.* Stoke on Trent: Trentham Books

Bancroft, S (2006) A child's work: the importance of fantasy play. *ReFocus Journal* 2 p28

Bancroft, S. Fawcett, M. Hay, P. (2004, 2005, and 2007) *5x5x5=creativity evaluation reports.* Bath: 5x5x5=creativity

Brain, J (2006) In the best interests of children. *ReFocus Journal* 2 p20-23

Bruce, T (1991) *Time to play in early childhood education.* London: Hodder and Stoughton

Burnard, P (2006) Provocations in creativity research. In L Bresler (ed) *International Handbook of Research in Arts Education* (p2003-2015). Dordrecht: Springer

Burnard, P, Grainger, T and Craft, A (2006) Documenting possibility thinking: A journey of collaborative enquiry. *International Journal of Early Years Education, Special Issue on Creativity and Cultural Innovation in Early Childhood Education* 14(3) p243-262

Carr, M (2001) *Assessment in Early Childhood Settings: Learning Stories.* London: Paul Chapman

Carr, M and Claxton, G (2004) A framework for teaching learning: the dynamics of disposition. *Early Years* 24(1)

Carse, J P (1987) *Finite and infinite games.* New York: Random House Publishers

Carson, R (1998, first published in 1965) *The Sense of Wonder.* New York: HarperCollins Publishers

Craft, A (2000) *Creativity Across the Primary Curriculum: Framing and Developing Practice.* London: Routledge.

Craft, A (2002) *Creativity and the Early Years: A Lifewide Foundation.* London: Continuum

Craft, A (2003) Creative thinking in the early Years of education. *Early Years* 23(2)

Craft, A (2003) The limits to creativity in education: dilemmas for the educator. *British Journal of Education Studies* 51(2)

Craft, A (2005) *Creativity in Schools: Tensions and Dilemmas.* London: Routledge

Craft, A, Cremin, T, Burnard, P and Chappell, K (2007) Teacher stance in creative learning: A study of progression. *Thinking Skills and Creativity* 2(1)

Craft, A, Cremin, T; and Burnard, P (eds) (2008) *Creative learning 3-11 and how we document it.* Stoke on Trent: Trentham Books

Craft, A, Gardner, H, Claxton, G. (Eds) (2008) *Creativity, Wisdom and Trusteeship. Exploring the Role of Education.* Thousand Oaks: Corwin Press

Craft, A, Jeffrey, B and Liebling, M (eds.) (2001) *Creativity Across the Primary Curriculum.* London: Continuum

Cremin, T, Burnard, P and Craft, A (2006) Pedagogy and possibility thinking in the early years. *Thinking Skills and Creativity* 1(2)

Cropley, A (2001) *Creativity in Education and Learning: A Guide for Teachers and Educators.* London: Kogan Page

Csikszentmihalyi, M (1997) *Creativity, Flow and the Psychology of Discovery and Invention.* London: Rider

Csikszentmihalyi, M. (2002) *Flow.* London: Rider

Dahlberg, G, Moss, P and Pence, A (1999) *Beyond Quality in Early Childhood Education and Care: Postmodern Perspectives.* London: Falmer Press

Dahlberg, G and Moss, P (2006) 'Introduction: our Reggio Emilia' in Rinaldi, C *In Dialogue with Reggio Emilia.* London: Routledge

Department for Education and Skills (2006) *Every Child Matters.* London: Department for Education and Skills

Doddington, M and Hilton, M (2007) *Child-centred Education: Reviving the Creative Tradition.* London: Sage

Drummond, MJ (2005) *Learning Bulletin Number 2: Pioneers in Creative Learning: Challenge and Change.* London: NESTA (National Endowment for Science, Technology and the Arts)

Duffy, B (2006) *Supporting creativity and imagination in the early years.* Buckingham: Open University

Dweck, C (2006) *Mindset: the new psychology of success.* New York: Ballantyne Books

Edwards, C Gandini, L and Forman, G (1998) *The Hundred Languages of Children – Advanced Reflections.* Greenwich, Connecticut: Ablex Publishing

Fawcett, M and Hay, P (2003) *5x5x5=creativity in the Early Years.* Bath and North East Somerset Council

Fawcett M and Hay P (2004) 5x5x5=Creativity in the Early Years. *The International Journal of Art and Design Education* 23(3)

Fisher, R. (2003) *Teaching Thinking.* London: Continuum

Gandini, L, Hill, L, Cadwell, L and Schwall, C (2005) *In the Spirit of the Studio: Learning from the Atelier of Reggio Emilia.* New York and London: Teachers College Press

Gardner, H, (1999) *Frames of mind.* Harvard University Press

Giudici, C, Rinaldi, C and Krechevsky, M (2001) *Making Learning Visible: Children as individual and group learners.* Cambridge MA and Reggio Emilia: Project Zero and Reggio Children

Gopnik, A, Meltzoff, A and Kuhl, P (1999) *How babies think: the science of childhood.* London: Weidenfeld and Nicholson

Gussin Paley, V (2004) *A Child's Work: The Importance of Fantasy Play.* University of Chicago Press

Harrington, D. M (1990) 'The Ecology of Human Creativity: A psychological perspective', in Runco, M A and Albert, R S (eds.) *Theories of Creativity.* London: Sage

Hart, S., Dixon, A., Drummond, MJ., and McIntyre, D. (2004) *Learning Without Limits.* Maidenhead: Open University Press

Hay, P (2001) *Making Art Work Report.* Bath and North East Somerset Council

Jeffrey, B and Woods, P (2003) *The Creative School.* London: Falmer Press

Jeffrey, B and Craft, A (2004) Teaching Creatively and Teaching for Creativity: distinctions and relationships. *Educational Studies* 30(1)

Jewitt, C and Kress K (eds) (2003) *Multimodal Literacy.* New York: Peter Lang

Katz, L (1994) *Reflections on the Reggio Emilia Approach.* Pennsylvania: Perspectives from ERIC/ EECE

Kline, N (1998) *Time to Think: Listening to ignite the human mind.* London: Cassell

Koestler, A (1999) *The Act of Creation.* Harmondsworth: Penguin

Kofman, F and Senge, P (2001) *The heart of learning organisations.* MA: MIT Center for Organisational Learning

Kolbe, U (2005) *It's Not a Bird Yet: The Drama of Drawing.* Byron Bay, Australia: Peppinot Press

Laevers, F (1994) *The Leuven Involvement Scale for Young Children.* Leuven, Belgium: Centre for Experiential Education

Laevers, F (2000a) Forward to the basics! Deep-level-learning and the experiential approach. *Early Years Journal* 20(2)

Laevers, F (2000b) *A process orientated child monitoring system for young children.* Leuven, Belgium: Centre for Experiential Education

Malaguzzi, L (1993) For an education based on relationships. *Young Children*, National Association for the Education of Young Children 49(1)

Malaguzzi, L (1996) *The Hundred Languages of Children* (Exhibition Catalogue) Reggio Emilia: Reggio Children

Mason, E and Duckett, R (2006) The life of an idea. *ReFocus Journal* 2

Matthews, J (1999) *The Art of Childhood and Adolescence: The Construction of Meaning.* London: Falmer

Matthews, J (2003) *Drawing and painting; children and visual representation.* (2nd edition) London: Paul Chapman Publishing

McNiff, J and Whitehead, J (2002) *Action Research: Principles and Practice.* London: Routledge

Moss, P (2003) *Beyond Caring: the case for reforming the childcare and early years workforce.* London: Daycare Trust

Moss, P (2006) *Contesting early childhood... and opening for change.* Thomas Coram Research Unit. Institute of Education, University of London

NACCCE (1999) *All our Futures: Creativity, Culture and Education.* London: DEE and DCMS

Nutbrown, C (1994) *Threads of Thinking: Young Children Learning and the Role of Early Education.* London: Paul Chapman Publishing

Oddie, D and Allen, G (1998) *Artists in Schools. A review.* London: The Stationery Office

Ouvry, M (2000) *Exercising Muscles and Minds: Outdoor play and the early years curriculum.* London: National Early Years Network

Pollard, A (2002) *Readings in Reflective Teaching.* London: Continuum

Pullman, Philip, Common sense has much to learn from moonshine. In *The Guardian* 22 January 2005

Qualification and Curriculum Authority (2000) *Guidance for the Foundation Stage.* London: Department for Education and Employment

Reiss, V and Pringle, E (2003) The Role of Artists in Sites for Learning. *International Journal of Art and Design Education* Volume 22(2)

Rinaldi, C (1998) The thought that sustains educational action on www.sightlines-initiative.com and originally in *Rechild* (April 1998)

Rinaldi, C (2001) In Giudici, C, Rinaldi, C. with Krechevsky, M *Making Learning Visible: children as individual and group learners*. Cambridge MA and Reggio Emilia: Project Zero and Reggio Children

Rinaldi, C and Moss, P (2004) 'What is Reggio?' in *Children in Europe* 6

Rinaldi, C (2006) *In dialogue with Reggio: listening, researching and learning*. Oxford: Routledge

Roberts, P (2006) *Nurturing Creativity in Young People*. Lonodn: DCMS

Robinson, K (2001) *Out of Our Minds: Learning To Be Creative*. Oxford: Capstone

Schön, D (1987) *Educating the Reflective Practitioner: Toward a new design for teaching and learning in the professions*. San Franciso: Jossey Bass

Siraj-Blatchford, I, Sylva, K, Muttock, S, Gilden, R and Bell, D (2002) *Effective Pedagogy in the Early Years: Researching Effective Pedagogy in the Early Years*. London: Department for Education and Skills Research Report 356

Snowber, C (2005) The mentor as artist: a poetic exploration of listening, creating and mentoring. *Mentoring and Tutoring* 13(3)

Souness, D and Fairley, R (2005) Room 13 in Atkinson, D and Nash, P (eds) *Social and critical practices in art education*. Stoke on Trent: Trentham Books

Steers and Swift (1999) A Manifesto for Art in Schools, Directions, *International Journal of Art and Design Education* 18(1)

Taylor, I (1975) An emerging view of creative actions, in Taylor, I. and Getzels, J. (eds.) *Perspectives in Creativity*. Chicago: Aldine

Trevarthen, C (2006) 'Doing' education – to know what others know. *Early Education Journal* 49

Vygotsky, L S (1978) *Mind in Society*. Cambridge: Mass: Harvard University Press

White, C (2007) *5x5x5 evaluation report for Wiltshire Local Authority*. Bath: 5x5x5=creativity

Young, S (2003) *Music with the Under-fours*. London: Routledge Falmer

Young, S and Glover, J (1998) *Music in the Early Years*. Abingdon, Oxon: Routledge Falmer

Websites

http://www.5x5x5creativity.org.uk

http://www.sightlines-initiative.com

http://www.pz.harvard.edu/mlv/

http://www.nesta.org.uk

Index